# MALE FRAUD

Understanding Sexual Harassment,
Date Rape, and Other Forms of
Male Hostility towards Women

## by
## Michael Anthony Corey

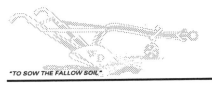

"TO SOW THE FALLOW SOIL"

PENNYWELL DRIVE . P.O. BOX 90883 . NASHVILLE, TENNESSEE 37209

WINSTON-DEREK
Publishers, Inc.

First printing

PUBLISHED BY WINSTON-DEREK PUBLISHERS, INC.
Nashville, Tennessee 37205

Library of Congress Catalog Card No: 91-68093
ISBN: 1-55523-506-9

Printed in the United States of America

To Nahia

# Table of Contents

# Acknowledgements

I would like to thank Mike and Jeanette Corey, Nahia, Beth, Johnny, Danny, Zig, Hyde, Greg, Kevin, Ernest, Janice, Sharyl, Mary, Charlotte, Bonnie, Ellen, Julie, Elizabeth, Lorraine, Claire, Valinda, Helene, Deborah, and the Lewises for their encouragement throughout the writing of this book.

Also, many thanks to Eli, Tina, Tamara, Elliot, Gina, Brandon, Joyce, Robbie, Aunt Sue, and all the Namays, who collectively helped to further my awareness of the many problems that are associated with male chauvinism.

# Introduction

IT WAS AN INTERESTING OPENING NIGHT IN HOLLYWOOD for the Andrew Dice Clay film *The Adventures of Ford Fairlane*. Instead of the movie opening to a round of critical adulation, or at least non-descript anonymity, it was befouled by the hurling of stink bombs by radical feminists, opposed to the "preposterous" antics of the film's infamous star.

Although the film itself was not nearly as "anti-woman" as expected, Clay's comedy routine *is* viciously anti-woman, or at least appears to be, and it is this hard-core reputation that has influenced his film. Although the man behind the routine, Andrew Clay Silverstein, claims that "the Diceman" is merely a character, and so is not indicative of his true feelings, millions of women all over the country continue to be thoroughly offended by his on-stage jeers and cuts, largely because they fail to see how or why anyone would be so lewd and crude toward women, even in a comedial atmosphere, unless somewhere deep inside they really felt that way.

In fact, when Clay was recently invited to host an episode of "Saturday Night Live," singer Sinead O'Connor and one of the show's female co-stars felt strongly enough about Clay's remarks to boycott the entire episode. Although this action had the predictable effect of vastly increasing the show's ratings (making it one of the most watched Saturday Night Lives ever), it nevertheless let the world know how strongly many women (and men) feel about Clay's brand of anti-woman humor.

Never before has one man been able to so galvanize the passions of such a huge contingent of the nation's citizenry. The fact that the promulgator of this extreme outcry is a comedian, and not a minister or lecturing professor, shows how deep and passionate our feelings tend to be in the highly sensitive area of male-female relations.

However, it is the male response towards Clay, not the female response, that is the most intriguing aspect of his enormous success. After all, it is only natural for women to band together to oppose a man who seems to be rubbing their noses into the dirt. What is unusual is that so many men seem to enjoy, and even identify with, Clay's remarks. When one takes the time to listen to Clay's comedy routine, one can't help but notice how popular his words are with his audience, which tends to be largely comprised of men. At least in terms of his ardent admirers, Clay is almost revered. These individuals memorize the Diceman's most notorious lines (especially his lewd nursery rhymes), and then chant them out at Clay's sold-out concerts. Even children as young as nine and ten are memorizing Clay's filthy lines and reciting them to one another (a truly disturbing prospect).

Given this unprecedented popularity, one can't help but conclude that Clay has struck a resonant chord in millions of people from coast to coast. No matter how lewd and vulgar he may be, hoards of people still love him. They love him because he actually says out loud what they seem to be feeling deep inside. While they may be too embarrassed or scared to say these things themselves in their own daily lives, they can derive vicarious enjoyment by listening to the Diceman.

At the same time, though, millions of women (and men) despise the very ground that Clay walks on. This is an interesting phenomenon, because one would think that anyone who is bad enough for millions of people to hate would also be bad enough for most everyone to hate. Yet such is clearly not the case. Millions of men (and some women) love Clay's comedy routine, while millions of women (and some men) detest it. This rough drawing of party lines along the classical male/female gender distinction is an indication that we are dealing here with problems that are largely gender-based in origin. Furthermore, the extreme bipolar response that Clay elicits on the part of so many people is a sure sign that we are dealing with one of the foundational problems of human existence: the time-honored conflict between the sexes.

The root cause of this gender-based conflict can be traced to the tremendous amount of hostility that millions of men feel towards women. This hostility is clearly reflected in the frightening number of male crimes against women that take place on a daily basis, both in this country and throughout the world. In this country alone a rape[1] is said to occur every six minutes, each and every day of the year, and a domestic beating is said to occur every eighteen seconds. With statistics like these, it is no wonder that 38 percent of all women in America will be sexually assaulted at some point in their lifetime.

As if this weren't enough, this hostility tends to spill over into other areas of life as well. The tragic consequence is that violent crimes of all kinds are typically driven by the male hostility response, both on a personal and a collective level. Humankind's unmistakable tendency to engage in warfare, for instance, can largely be traced to the utterly malignant nature of the male hostility response towards women, as can most other forms of male violence. Indeed, this hostility is so great that it isn't even being restricted to humans, since violent environmental crimes of all kinds are now being committed against Mother Earth herself and all her subhuman inhabitants, the tragic consequence of which is that we may no longer have a viable planet to live on in the not-so-distant future.

It is for these reasons that the male hostility response toward women, as personified by Andrew Dice Clay, must be considered as one of the most important problems facing our society today. It may even be the most important problem of all, because hostility-prone men run the world and have direct access to the most frightening weapons of mass destruction ever concocted. Hence, an unchecked male hostility response can easily lead to the worst nightmare of them all: nuclear war.

Ironically, though, a great many of these women-hating men don't outwardly seem to hate women at all. If anything, they seem to *love* them profusely. This is the first way in which women-hating men are fraudulent: they outwardly act as if they love women, when in fact they hate them deep inside, often profusely. We will be exploring the reason for this contradictory state of affairs throughout the remainder of this book.

### Goal
The goal of this book is threefold:
1) to discover where the male hostility response towards women ultimately comes from,
2) to understand the function it serves in the male psychological economy, and
3) to learn how it can be overcome once and for all.

In order to find the answers to these questions, we must first turn to an important concept known as the Macho Ideal.

# The Macho Ideal

ALMOST ALL MEN IN THIS COUNTRY ARE RAISED TO BELIEVE in an unspoken code of ethics, which I have termed the *Macho Ideal*, that specifies what it means to be a "real man." This sociological credo determines to a large extent how a man is "supposed" to treat the members of the opposite sex.

Although the specific contents of the Macho Ideal are rarely discussed openly, they form an exceedingly powerful influence upon a man's subconscious mind, and in fact permeate virtually all aspects of our modern-day life. Indeed, the Macho Ideal is so all-encompassing that it determines the behavioral ground rules for virtually every aspect of a susceptible man's life in the world. Thus, in order to understand why so many men feel such hate and hostility toward women, we must first attempt to gain an understanding of the origin and nature of the Macho Ideal in men.

The roots of the Macho Ideal can be traced back to the very origins of our patriarchal (male-dominated) society many thousands of years ago. Although a few cultures in the past have had their power structures centered around women (and hence were matriarchal), the vast majority of cultures have had their power structures centered around men. We can conclude from this historical fact that patriarchy represents the natural tendency of most human societies.

Dominant patriarchal societies can be seen to have originated by the simple fact that men tend to be physically bigger and stronger overall than women. This is a natural "given" that the first patriarchal males chose to deal with in a very predictable fashion: they naturally internalized their size and strength advantage over females into their innermost psychological makeup, which in turn led them to develop a society that was centered around men instead of women. Unfortunately, it also resulted in an extreme emphasis on the more physical and aggressive aspects of human behavior, especially in the male.

University of California at San Diego psychologist Warren Farrell agrees that the origins of our patriarchal society can be traced to the physical differences between the sexes. According to Farrell, people in prehistoric societies rarely lived into their thirties, so females hardly had time for anything else besides getting pregnant and raising children. This caused them to be particularly vulnerable to attack from roving male predators. As a consequence, in order to secure protection for both themselves and their children, these prehistoric women were forced to use sex to "buy" protection from "friendly" male killers, who agreed to exchange sexual favors for physical protection. Eventually, this type of relationship between the sexes translated into entire societies that were centered around the interests of violent and aggressive males, at the expense of more submissive females.

Today, although our society is much more "cultured" and "sophisticated" overall, our social structure still reveals its prehistoric patriarchal roots. Patriarchal men still ultimately rely on their physical size and power advantage to dominate the women in their lives, although in our "modern" world more indirect means (such as the established social order) are typically used to carry out this domination.

### Physiological Gender Asymmetries and the Origin of Patriarchal Societies

It is a well-known fact that the male sex hormone testosterone strongly reinforces any preexisting aggressive tendencies in men, through the many psychological and physiological effects that it is known to have on male behavior. Numerous studies, for instance, have indicated a strong positive correlation between aggressive behavior in males and blood testosterone levels. Indeed, testosterone may even be partially responsible for generating aggressive tendencies in women as well, who also manufacture varying amounts of this important hormone in their adrenal glands.

When the size, strength, and hormonal asymmetries between men and women are duly considered, it suddenly becomes easy to see why patriarchal societies (via male allegiance to the Macho Ideal) developed as they did. When naive, philosophically ignorant males are presented with bodies and hormones that allow them, on the whole, to be so much stronger and more aggressive than females, we would naturally expect them to feel and act superior in almost every conceivable way.

Indeed, given the human mind's extraordinary capacity for generalization during the early childhood process of attitude development, wherein an individual's entire cognitive stance is typically built on a few fundamental assumptions, we would naturally expect the male feeling of superiority to be intimately involved in virtually every aspect of a man's cognitive and behavioral life, since by the age of five or six the assumptions of the Macho Ideal have become dispersed throughout a young boy's entire mind. This explains why it is so difficult to get a true macho-oriented male to see his own conceptual and behavioral error: because virtually his entire character and self-image is based on this faux pas. Thus, an explicit admission of error for the genuinely macho individual is tantamount to an all-encompassing act of self-negation, which itself carries the subconscious connotation of psychological suicide.

Once this body-based feeling of superiority originally took root in the minds of the first "real" men, it was only a matter of time until entire patriarchal societies were built around it.[2] These patriarchal societies, of course, contained within themselves the pedagogical tools for the own self-propagation, through the automatic perpetuation of their underlying philosophical credo, the Macho Ideal. Through a variety of subtle and not-so-subtle techniques, these patriarchal societies developed methods for instilling the fundamentals of the Macho Ideal into their children, well before the first birthday. As these youngsters were continually weaned on the various precepts of the Macho Ideal throughout their childhood and adolescent years, the vast majority of them couldn't help but internalize these values in their minds by the time they became adults. Typically, a full "conversion" was obtained by the age of five or six. From this crucial point onward, it was only a matter of time until these macho precepts came to be involved in every aspect of their lives.

What we see happening, then, in *all* patriarchal societies is a self-replicating process of self-preservation, whose chief purpose is the maintainance of male domination at all cost. The societal instrument for the attainment of this end is an extreme emphasis upon the dictates of the Macho Ideal throughout all stages of the socialization process, from birth to old age.

It is a remarkable thought indeed to realize that the immense power of patriarchal societies is a natural consequence of the simple biological fact that men tend to be bigger, stronger, and more aggressive overall than women. Today, of course, we know that mere size and strength have little or nothing to do with a person's overall competence as a human being, especially in the context of our modern technological society.[3] In prehistoric times, though, a person's physical prowess was much more important, for two reasons: 1) his or her survival actually depended on it, and 2) much less demand was made upon the mind's higher, intellectual faculties at that time, due to the relatively unsophisticated nature of all prehistoric societies. Hence, it should come as no surprise that patriarchal societies developed as they did, given the gender-based physiological asymmetries that have always existed between the sexes.

3

## Components of the Macho Ideal

As we saw above, the superiority that was originally conferred upon men by their bigger, stronger, and more aggressive bodies naturally percolated over into the various psychological characteristics that have come to be identified with masculinity. Swiss psychiatrist C.G. Jung was the first to perform an extensive analysis of these gender-based psychological differences. The results of his analysis are now well known: although men and women share a large number of different psychological characteristics, certain qualities tend to be much more pronounced in one gender or the other.

For instance, although the propensity for cold, logical thought is present in both genders, it tends to be concentrated more in males. Similarly, although the propensity for nurturance and compassion is present in both genders, it tends to be concentrated more in females. Jung concluded from his repeated observations that there were both "masculine" and "feminine" personality characteristics in the human psyche. Among the naturally-occurring masculine characteristics, Jung cited controlled aggressiveness, logical thought, active creativity, psychological firmness, and a tendency to heroic, goal-oriented behavior. Among the naturally-occurring female characteristics, he cited integrative, synthetic thinking, compassion, patience, the capacity for interpersonal relationship, empathy, and love of life.[4] Interestingly enough, each of these respective personality characteristics can be shown to be related in some fashion to the various anatomical and physiological differences between the two sexes.[5] Thus, a man's inherent psychological tendencies further help to reinforce the behavioral dictates of the Macho Ideal.

The Macho Ideal itself appears to be based upon a composite conceptual amalgamation of the most prominent personality qualities that naturally appear in the male psyche, which have somehow coalesced together to form a single overall world view. It is worth noting, however, that this "macho" world view isn't the direct (and therefore inevitable) result of these naturally-occurring male characteristics per se. Rather, it is the indirect result of prehistoric man's naive conceptual *extrapolation* about what these qualities should imply for a man's overall life in the world, i.e., it is the result of an ignorant extension of these intrinsically neutral qualities in the direction of prehistoric man's basest animal impulses (the desire for nihilism and complete domination over others).

**4**

Now we are in a position to consider the individual conceptual components of the Macho Ideal. These include the following:

1. A general feeling of superiority over women in virtually all "worthwhile" aspects of human life.
2. The conviction that "might makes right."
3. The belief that male happiness should take precedence over female happiness.
4. The belief in absolute independence from all possible sources of dependency in human life, especially those that involve women.
5. The belief that men should be more competent overall in the bedroom than women.
6. The belief that women are simply important ingredients in a man's constellation of "fulfillment" factors, not equally important individuals who deserve equal access to the various opportunities for happiness and fulfillment in life.

All of these beliefs seem to have grown out of the size, strength, and hormonal asymmetries that naturally occur between the sexes. It is as if the original believers in the Macho Ideal said to themselves:

"We are naturally bigger, stronger, and more aggressive than most of the members of the opposite sex. We were given these advantages by the powers that rule the heavens. Therefore, we are not only supposed to *have* these advantages; we are supposed to *exploit* them as much as we possibly can in our own personal lives. As a result, we deserve preferential treatment over women in all of our endeavors, because bigger and stronger is better and more important. Period."

This kind of outdated world view is clearly pathological and unrealistic. Yet, millions of men around the world desperately cling to it, in spite of all the destructive consequences that naturally go along with it.

This is the second[6] way in which the macho-oriented male is fraudulent: he aspires to a goal that is illegitimately produced, impossible to attain, and immoral to strive for. Therefore, he is constantly striving to be something he isn't (and can never be), and this is fraudulent by definition.

**5**

Fortunately, the Macho Ideal is "just" a belief. Like all beliefs, it is subject to error. However, it is also subject to rational revision as well. This gives us some reason for hope as far as the future of the human race is concerned.

# The Dynamical Relationship
# Between the Sexes

IT IS A WELL-KNOWN FACT THAT IN MOST SEXUALLY-ORIENTED heterosexual relationships, the male is typically the one who pursues the female in his often ceaseless attempt to gain sexual gratification. This fundamental dynamic between the sexes is found throughout the animal kingdom, where the males of most species are known to actively pursue the females for mating purposes.

Much of the reason for this curious behavior in humans can again be traced to the built-in anatomical and physiological differences between males and females. Due to the fundamental structure of the sexual act, males are called upon to insert their rigid sexual organ into the female's body, via her vaginal orifice. The male thus tends to assume an *active, penetrating* role during the act of copulation, while the female tends to assume a much more *passive, receptive* role.

That is to say, the built-in anatomy and physiology of the male causes him to assume the aggressive position of wanting to physically insert his sexual organ into the woman's vaginal orifice, whereas the built-in anatomy and physiology of the female causes her to assume the more passive role of deciding whether or not to allow herself to be penetrated by her potential mate. Although it isn't physically mandatory that the male assume this more dominant, aggressive role during the sexual act, he is very much inclined to do so, given the naturally-occurring asymmetries between males and females we have discussed.

The male sex hormone testosterone—which, as we have already seen, helps to promote behavioral aggression—also figures prominently in this all-important sexual dynamic in three important ways:
1) it greatly facilitates the process of penile erection,
2) it vastly increases male sexual desire,[7] and
3) it helps to promote the aggressive behavior that is necessary if the male is to take the active role of wanting to pursue and penetrate the female's body.

This sexual dynamic, which sees the male aggressively pursuing the female in a wide variety of species, is actually so important and pervasive in human affairs that it tends to become generalized over into non-sexual areas as well. This can be seen in virtually all aspects of male-female social behavior, from the time-honored ritual of the man asking the woman for her hand in marriage, to the frightening male belligerence seen in rape. In both of these cases, and many more like them, it is the man who characteristically (though certainly not always) pursues the woman, and it is the woman who, at least initially, is in the position of deciding whether or not she wants to participate in the male's proposed course of action.[8] *This fundamental behavioral paradigm can be seen to have originated directly from the physiologically-induced behavior differences that typically result during the sexual act between men and women.*

It is precisely here with this exceedingly important interpersonal dynamic that an important source of male hostility toward women can be found. For as long as the male occupies the role of the sexual pursuer, he is much more likely to become physically and emotionally frustrated, either when he cannot reach the woman he is pursuing, or when he is actually rejected by her outright. This frustration is compounded by the fact that the male tends to experience significantly more sexual urgency and excitement during the initial "chase" scene than the female does, since the testosterone circulating in the male's blood enables him to get far more excited far more quickly than females typically do.[9]

When these two factors are considered together, we see that males can potentially experience far more anger and frustration than females when their urgent request for a sexual union with a woman is flatly denied. With some men, this possibility of physical and emotional frustration is so intensely unpleasant that they often live in almost perpetual fear of it; indeed, some men have actually gone so far as to *never* sexually pursue women for this very reason. This is why men are capable of feeling so much hate and hostility toward women when their bold sexual offers are finally turned down after a prolonged "chase scene": not only are their macho egos severely damaged by the rejection, their erections must go through the often painful process of self-dissipation without sexual release.

Interestingly enough, there is a physiological basis for a man's profound discomfort after unrequited love. In preparation for immanent ejaculation, the various internal components of the male sexual apparatus—the testicles, epididymi, prostate, and seminal vesicle—all become "pumped up" and engorged with their respective sexual fluids. However, when ejaculation does not occur, these fluids must stagnate within the body, and this in turn can cause tenderness, pain, and infection in the testicles, prostate, and epididymi. There is even a legitimate urological diagnosis of this condition known as "blue balls."

So a man's discomfort after a sexual rejection is much more than just "in his head." As Jeff, a jazz musician, once described it, the cumulative effect of this sexual denial for him is like "chasing hopefully at a constantly receding target, and then, once the target has finally stopped receding, running full speed ahead into a brick wall."

It isn't surprising that many males are enraged by this unpleasant experience, some so much so that they will do almost anything to avoid it, even if it means forcing the sexual act upon an unwilling victim. This is surely one of the causative factors in "date rape," where males with little or no self-control tend to get so excited with their own dates that they get carried away into raping them.

### Preventing Date Rape

If you are a woman, one of the most effective ways of preventing date rape is to never lead a man on in a sexual fashion if you're not planning to go to bed with him. In this way, you can prevent him from getting a running start at getting sexually excited. The logic here is that if he doesn't get turned on to begin with, he won't have to be "turned off" when you say "no" to his sexual advances. In this way, when you do say "no" to him, his feeling of rejection probably won't be enough to knock him (or you) senseless.

At all times, though, you should remember that most men tend to get sexually far more quickly, and with far less stimulation, than most women. Sometimes all it takes is a sexy glance to drive a man sexually crazy. So be careful. And don't allow yourself to get in a situation where you *could* get "pawed on," or potentially raped.

If you follow these precautions religiously, you should be pretty safe (provided you haven't chosen to go out with a highly motivated rapist). As always, though, there is a risk that a woman will be raped whenever she steps out of the house, so perpetual vigilance is a must, even in familiar surroundings. It is a tragic reminder of the brutal and heartless times in which we live.

# Sex, Hostility, and the Macho Ideal

ACCORDING TO PSYCHOLOGISTS AND SEX THERAPISTS, there is a strong element of hostility that can potentially exist throughout all stages of the sexual process. In this chapter we will explore the relationship of this hostility response to the sexual act itself.

### Male Hostility in Light of the Sexual Performance Asymmetries Between Men and Women

In terms of their God-given inalienable rights as human beings, men and women may indeed have been created equal. It would be a mistake to assume, however, that men and women are absolutely equivalent when it comes down to their fundamental strengths and capacities in life. They are not. Indeed, men and women are not equivalent *by definition*, otherwise they would be identical to one another, and therefore of the same gender. While they may be *equal* in terms of their fundamental rights as human beings, they most certainly are not equal or equivalent in terms of their gender-based talents and capacities.

This is especially true when we consider the intrinsic differences between each gender's physiological sex drive. On this one important point, the two sexes were most definitely *not* created "equal" at all. To think otherwise is to remain ignorant of the tremendous amount of scientific information that has been accumulated in recent years about human sexuality, which shows conclusively that the intrinsic differences in sex drives between men and women extend far beyond the range of mere anatomical differences. What we're talking about here are major differences in sexual *performance* between the two genders.

It is a well-known fact, for instance, that men and women tend to reach their respective sexual peaks at different times during the life cycle. Men tend to reach their sexual peak during the late teens and early twenties, whereas women tend to reach their sexual peak much later, during the early to mid-thirties, and sometimes even extending to the early forties.[10]

A number of other differences in sexual performace are also known to exist between the two genders. Over 25 years ago Masters and Johnson[11] conducted a series of pioneering studies which showed that not only do men and women tend to get sexually excited at different rates, they also tend to *remain* excited for different periods of time as well. Not surprisingly, they found that men tend to get sexually excited far more quickly than women, and that once they become excited, men tend to experience significantly greater urgency in getting their sexual tensions released than women do. The researchers also found that men are able to maintain this high level of sexual excitement for a much shorter duration of time overall as well, due to the fact that a man's level of sexual arousal tends to plummet after ejaculation occurs. Indeed, once vaginal penetration has taken place, some men are able to remain aroused for only a few seconds before ejaculation occurs (hence the problem of "premature ejaculation"). Finally, Masters and Johnson found that once orgasm transpires in the male, there is almost complete satiation (albeit temporarily).

Women, on the other hand, were found by the researchers to be far slower in their capacity to get initially excited, at least in comparison to the response times displayed by most men. Modern studies have confirmed this finding: whereas a mere glance from a woman may be enough to turn a man on sexually, the same sort of minimal stimulus is usually *not* sufficient to bring most women to the same degree of sexual excitement. This is why foreplay is such an important ingredient in the genesis of the female sexual response: because women tend to require a comparatively large degree of stimulation in order to reach an optimal level of sexual excitement. At the same time, though, the greater volatility of the male sex drive often causes a man to inadvertently reach orgasm during the initial period of foreplay. This is due to the fact that the amount of stimulation required to fully arouse most women tends to be more than sufficient to bring most men to orgasm.

Once a woman finally becomes optimally aroused, her sexual capacity seems to follow the pattern of a long and drawn-out *plateau*, instead of the rapid peak and sudden drop-off experienced by the majority of men. It is the female's native capacity for reaching multiple orgasms that makes this type of extended plateau possible. Indeed, many women possess the capacity for maintaining a truly *incredible* level of sexual arousal over *many* consecutive orgasms. By contrast, most men tend to burn out after a single orgasm, or at most, after two or three consecutive orgasms.

Interestingly enough, a large part of the reason why many men tend to feel some degree of hostility toward women seems to be related to this inherent sexual performance asymmetry between males and females. One of the underlying dictates of the Macho Ideal, as we have seen, is that a man should be the dominant force through all stages of the love-making process. Thus, when a given male finds that he can't "keep up" in the bedroom, his macho self-image (if he has one) tends to be shattered, and this often translates into outright hostility.

But it is the rare man indeed who can "keep pace" with an uninhibited woman who has been brought to full arousal. It is even more rare for a man to be capable of bringing a woman to *complete* satiation, where she no longer possesses the capacity to experience an additional orgasm. While a man may think that he has brought his (uninhibited) partner to complete satiation, more often than not this is because she has voluntarily given up her quest for more orgasms, in response to the prior exhaustion of her man.

Given this fundamental performance asymmetry between the sexes, it is the uninhibited woman who emerges as the "victor" in terms of orgasm intensity, number, and overall endurance. She only falters in terms of her relative slowness to become optimally excited in the beginning. In comparison, the only sexual "prize of distinction" that the man can claim for himself is his overall lustfulness and quickness to become excited: this includes the intensity of his feeling of sexual urgency, the relative quickness with which he reaches orgasm, and the tremendous satiation he obtains after a single ejaculation. In a sense, then, it is the male who is more "efficient" in the sexual arena, since he is the one who can usually obtain the greatest amount of pleasure in the shortest amount of time. Unfortunately, though, most men are not satisfied with this paltry distinction. This is because in the game of pleasure, it is commonly believed that the one who obtains the greatest amount of pleasure for the longest period of time is the one who comes out ahead in the end.

Objectively speaking, of course, it is ridiculous to speak of the inherent sexual capacities of males and females in terms of a physical contest to be "won" by one gender or the other. Sex should never be viewed in such a competitive manner. Period. According to the dictates of the Macho Ideal, however, sex *is* a potentially competitive activity, since it seems to reflect back on the intrinsic capacities of its participants. And since the Macho Ideal says that men are supposed to be superior to women in all relevant aspects of human life, especially in the sexual sphere, those who faithfully adhere to this macho standard often can't help but view sex in this antiquated manner.

It is for this reason that the male perception of female superiority in the bedroom tends to cause a hidden inferiority complex in those males who most rigidly subscribe to the dictates of the Macho Ideal. It is a humbling experience indeed when the macho man realizes that, in

**13**

terms of his overall sexual intensity and endurance, he is largely inferior to the members of the opposite sex, whom he has been taught to believe are inferior to him in virtually every conceivable way. It is evident to him that something somewhere must be wrong, but he just can't bring himself to admit that it has anything to do with him or his own standard of masculinity. At the same time, though, the reality of his own perceived inferiority in the bedroom repeatedly stares him in the face. Even so, he *still* can't face the idea that his antiquated standard of masculinity may be wrong. As a consequence, he unconsciously chooses to become angry. He becomes angry at not being the privileged person he originally thought he was, and at the audacity of the real world to mock the precious standard of masculinity that he was raised to believe in.

This is where a sizable proportion of the hatred that many men feel towards women actually comes from. When a genuinely macho individual finally comes to the realization that he is repeatedly being outclassed by the opposite sex in bed, his belief in the Macho Ideal suddenly comes under severe attack. This attack is so severe, in fact, that it forces him to make a critical (though unconscious) choice: to either give up his overall allegiance to the Macho Ideal, or to defend it to the end by being hostile and aggressive in his day-to-day behavior, especially to those "overly ambitious" women who are responsible for generating this severe threat to his machismo.

This subliminal decision seems like a classic no-win scenario to him: if he chooses to give up his allegiance to the Macho Ideal, he feels like he will lose his masculinity and turn into a "wimpy faggot"; on the other hand, if he chooses to defend this allegiance by being overly hostile and aggressive, he risks being labeled a bully, or even worse, losing control and getting arrested or killed. This is the ultimate question that separates the *real* men from the *faggot* boys: any *real* man would clearly choose the hostility alternative over the voluntary relinquishing of his precious masculinity.

The obvious fallacy in this apparent "either-or" dilemma is that one does *not* have to give up one's masculinity or avowed heterosexuality if one chooses to give up one's allegiance to the Macho Ideal. One simply has to give up belief in the false and overly pathological characterization of masculinity that the Macho Ideal has wrongly been spelling out in human affairs for centuries. In its place, one can begin believing in a brand new characterization of masculinity, which emphasizes the freedom of the male to pursue the very best aspects of human experience, including emotionality, creativity, sincerity, peacefulness, and an undying commitment to maximizing the good in life, regardless of cost. Clearly this new definition of masculinity frees one up from the extremely repressive yoke of the old masculine order, so that, after a lifetime of slavery to an antiquated value system, one can finally enjoy the very best that life has to offer, without fear of losing one's masculinity in the process. *It is for this reason we can say that this conceptual emancipation from the old Macho Ideal constitutes the ultimate form of personal and spiritual liberation for the modern-day American male.*

Unfortunately, it is exceedingly difficult for the genuinely macho individual to come to the above realization. It seems like blasphemy to him, so he refuses to take it seriously. This is the same sort of individual who is deeply threatened by the superior sexual capacities of the opposite sex. No one wants to have their inner sense of security (mistaken though it may be) threatened by anyone or anything. After all, it is human nature to crave security, and to do anything within reason to obtain it. The problem, however, with the macho brand of security desired by "real" men is twofold:

1) it is an intrinsically impossible goal to attain, no matter how hard one tries, and

2) it must be striven for at the expense of the opposite sex, through the use of various hostile means for defending the dictates of the Macho Ideal.

It is for these reasons that we can judge this type of macho-oriented security to be inadequate, inferior, and even immoral overall.

### Impotence

It has been estimated that one out of every five men will experience chronic sexual impotence at some point in their adult lives. Although physical problems are to blame in many of these cases, the majority seem to be due almost exclusively to psychological factors.

An important clue to the origin of "psychological impotence" can be found in the way that the macho male tends to view this problem. The fact is, impotence is perhaps the most humiliating thing that can ever happen to a macho male. It directly contradicts everything he stands for in his life and everything he believes about himself.

As we have seen, it is his physical superiority over the members of the opposite sex which is the *sine qua non* of the macho man's all-important self-image. This physical superiority of course extends to the sexual arena most of all, since the Macho Ideal dictates that the man is

**15**

to be the dominant force over every aspect of the sexual act, especially in the crucial area of generating and maintaining an erection. Sex, naturally enough, is impossible in the absence of an erection, so the chief responsibility for making sex possible, at least in the beginning, must inevitably fall upon the man.

This is why impotence is one of the most feared things in a macho man's life: it represents an across-the-board negation of everything he happens to believe about himself. As a consequence, it adds up to the ultimate humiliation: the complete negation of his own self-image. Unfortunately, though, that which the macho man fears the most is that which is likely to come upon him at some point in his adult life, because it is based on a faulty premise: his own superiority over the opposite sex. In other words, the reason why the macho man cannot deal with the prospect of his own impotence is because he insists on viewing it as a general loss of his own manhood, which itself is predicated on the male's general superiority over the female. Hence, if it is a falsehood that men are superior overall to women, then the macho man's sense of his own manhood, which is itself based on this superiority, is bound to eventually fail as well. And since the most important symbol of this manhood—the ability to generate and maintain an erection—is based on this faulty premise, it too must fail under the ongoing stress and strain of modern existence. Like the proverbial house of cards that has been built on a weak foundation, a self-image that has been built on the myth of male superiority will inevitably collapse.

### Hope for the Impotent

If the above explanation for the etiology of psychological impotence is accurate, then this clinical entity would seem to be particularly amenable to cognitive restructuring therapy. That is to say, if psychologically-derived impotence is caused by a mistaken belief in male superiority which has unconsciously been fostered by the Macho Ideal, then a radical alteration in one's beliefs concerning the true meaning of manhood should help to alleviate this stubborn syndrome.

Thus, if a macho-oriented man who is suffering from impotence is able to come to a full awareness of the ridiculous and self-limiting nature of the Macho Ideal in all possible contexts (including his own personal one), he hopefully will be able to discard his belief in male superiority once and for all in favor of a more realistic and egalitarian view of the two sexes. If he is able to successfully do this, his sexual apparatus will then be under greatly reduced pressure to perform adequately. This in turn should free it up to perform more effectively in the face of all the stresses and strains of modern existence.

## Jumping Through Hoops

Given the extreme volatility of the male sex drive, which we noted earlier, along with the superior, privileged status that is conferred upon men by the Macho Ideal, it follows that most macho-oriented men *expect* their women to accommodate their idiosyncratic sexual needs with little or no resistance at all, regardless of how unusual or extreme these needs may happen to be. They even expect their women to actually be *happy* about serving them in this subordinated sexual capacity. After all, if the purpose of women in human society is supposed to be directly tied to their role in serving men, as the Macho Ideal says it should be, it follows that a "good" woman will do her very best to satisfy a man's sexual needs, regardless of the amount of self-abasement she must experience in order to do so.

Of course, in the real world, very few women actually live up to this idealistic standard. Even prostitutes expect financial compensation for their sexual favors. In fact, most women expect a man to go through some sort of special behavioral sequence before they will allow themselves to go to bed with him. The specific nature of these behaviors varies tremendously from woman to woman. Some women simply require a man to take them out to dinner or to buy them a gift before they will sleep with him. Others require a long-and-drawn-out courtship process before they will consent to the sexual act. Still others require a marriage license before they will take the big plunge (though this is certainly much less common now in America than it once was).

The man who has been schooled in the macho tradition, however, deeply resents having to jump through all of these hoops in order to get what he *really* wants out of a woman: sexual satisfaction. According to the Macho Ideal, you will recall, a man shouldn't *have* to jump through any hoops at all in order to go to bed with a woman, since he is supposed to be a privileged character in society. He honestly believes that women are supposed to do everything in their power to make their respective men happy; hence, he *expects* the woman of his choice to accommodate him sexually (and otherwise) with no reistance at all.

What this means is that the process of hoop-jumping in order to have sex with a woman amounts to still another violation of the Macho Ideal in the twisted mind of the susceptible individual. Indeed, for the man who identifies strongly with this pathological Ideal, the extent of

**17**

his hostility toward women tends to be *directly related* to how many hoops he is repeatedly forced to jump through before he is allowed to get what he wants from a woman: the more hoops, the more hostility. In fact, for some hard-core believers in the Macho Ideal, the very idea that they must be *allowed* to have sex by a *mere* woman often has the effect of infuriating them to the point of violence. A good many sex offenders clearly respond to women in this fashion.

Perhaps if the male sex drive weren't so powerful, or weren't so extraordinarily volatile, men wouldn't feel so resentful toward women when they are forced to jump through a series of hoops before they are allowed to get what they want. The fact is, however, that the male sex drive *is* this powerful, so some degree of conflict between macho men and their potential sex partners seems almost inevitable (unless the particular woman in question is so easy that she doesn't require any hoop-jumping at all from a man).

We mustn't forget that in the mind of the genuinely macho individual, the experience of being sexually excited without the immediate expectation of relief is *exceedingly* unpleasant. In fact, it is like dying of thirst in a world where all the water is possessed by women. In this kind of situation, of course, a person would be correct in expecting to be given water directly and unconditionally. But sex is a different story, since a man doesn't need sex in order to survive. The male sex drive may be strong, but it isn't *that* strong! Nevertheless, many men subjectively experience their level of sexual tension to *be* this intense. This is why those males who rigidly adhere to the dictates of the Macho Ideal *expect* to be able to reach sexual satiation with a woman with little or no hassle: they figure that if their inner sense of sexual urgency is *this* strong, and if women are supposed to serve men in all relevant areas of life, then a good woman should cater immediately to a man's sexual needs, whether she knows him very well or not.

Some men are so caught up in this level of thought that deep down they would like to see *any* woman go to bed with them, merely for the asking. This is the type of fantasy that typically occurs in the minds of avid consumers of pornography. These individuals repeatedly imagine themselves having wild sexual episodes with the voluptuous women in these magazines, even though they don't actually know them. This is quite easy to understand, because as far as the Macho Ideal is concerned, the question of whether or not a man actually knows a given woman should not enter into the question of whether they will actually have sex together; as long as he *wants* to have sex with her, the Macho Ideal dictates that he should be able to do so.

**18**

Of course, in the real world, this type of absolute sexual "freedom" rarely, if ever, occurs. This is why pornographic movies and magazines are so enormously popular: they capitalize on the internal male fantasy of unrestrained sexual access to all females, which again has been determined largely by the Macho Ideal.

Tragically, some men find it difficult to draw the line between fantasy and reality. After fantasizing for months or years about having sexual intercourse with a female (*any* female), a macho man may be unable to restrain himself when he finds himself actually out on a date with a real live woman. This is especially true if the woman has been a tease throughout the evening. By the end of the night, the aroused man may not be able to take no for an answer, and a date rape could be the result.

Date rape occurs because the date-rapist fully expects to be able to go to bed with a woman after jumping through a certain number of hoops. Unfortunately, it is his unsuspecting date who must pay for his lack of self-control.

### Sex and the "Real" Man

It is hard for many women to understand precisely how important sex is for most men. For millions of men throughout the world (especially those of an adolescent age or mentality), sex is so important that the physical act itself usually takes precedence over the identity of the person it is taking place with. When these males fantasize about sex, they typically don't fantasize about being with a certain person as much as they fantasize about *doing* certain *things* with whoever it is that they happen to be with. Indeed, to the extent that these men actually fantasize about being with a certain person, it is usually in terms of the *specific acts* that will be performed with that person, *not* in terms of being with that person as a person.

This kind of male tends to see sex as a kind of amusement park ride, in which it is the quality of the ride itself that counts, not the identity of the person it is ridden with. It is this type of macho individual that finds it relatively easy to have sex with a prostitute, since he is far more interested in *what* he does in bed than who he actually does it with. The fact that prostitutes don't come cheap doesn't seem to bother this kind of person at all, since he fully expects that true quality in any type of worthwhile endeavor will be expensive.

This is also the type of male who tends to find extramarital sex a completely justifiable activity. Because he is in it solely for the sex, he doesn't feel much guilt over it at all, since he still loves his wife just as much as ever. This is why he fully expects his wife to forgive him if and when he ever gets caught: because he only goes out on his wife "for the fun of it," and this seems to make it a relatively minor offense in his mind. In fact, this type of man actually expects his wife to look the other way when she finds out about his philandering, since, according to the Macho Ideal, she is supposed to *want* him to have a good time in his life!

This brand of male stands in stark contrast to the more romantic variety, who is far more interested in *who* he is with than in *what* he actually does in bed. Not only do these romantic individuals still exist in our society, their numbers actually seem to be growing. These are the men who like to fantasize about the quality of the love they want to experience in a single romantic relationship, not the "sexual decathlon" they want to engage in once they enter the bedroom.

Paradoxically, it is this type of romantic individual who seems to make the best lover overall. For in his quest to find the ultimate romance, he ends up performing better sexually than the more macho type of individual, who is in the bedroom solely for the sexual fireworks he thinks he can muster up.

### The Macho Ideal and the Archetype of the Whore

The Macho Ideal is so influential and pervasive in a (macho) man's life that it even helps to determine what kind of woman he finds sexually appealing. Naturally, we would expect him to desire a woman whose sexual qualities complement his own. These masculine qualities include, as one might expect, animalistic lustiness, physical aggressiveness, and athletic competency in the bedroom. As a consequence, it is to be expected that the macho-oriented male will desire a woman who is fully compatible with these masculine traits. But these are precisely the qualities that are exhibited by the whore, whose very nature is defined by her outrageously extreme sexuality. This is why so many macho-oriented males are turned on by "slutty" women: because this sluttiness directly complements the man's own inner machismo.[12]

The result of this complementarity is what the macho man has been looking for all along: the best possible time in the bedroom. These macho desires are reinforced by the typical male obsession with the sex act itself. Indeed, the male appetite for sex tends to be so overwhelming that many men are literally *obsessed* with finding the "perfect" woman for their bedroom fantasies.

Let us make no mistake here: the macho man has a definite behavioral agenda in mind when it comes to his idea of the perfect sexual experience, and he obviously wants to find the perfect woman to accomodate him in this capacity. Unfortunately, this tends to mean a slutty woman who is fully capable of "doing it all" in the bedroom. However, this isn't all the macho man wants. In addition to a wildly sexy female partner, he also wants a *nice* woman whom he can count on to be a good mother for his children. More often than not, this type of niceness is deemed to be incompatible with the physical sluttiness that he is also looking for. This is why so many "happily married men" end up getting involved with "loose" extramarital partners.

In other words, as Edward Dahlberg has pointed out, "what most men desire is a virgin who is [simultaneously] a whore."[13] This explains why so many married men are dissatisfied with their wives in the bedroom: because they want to *live* with a virgin but have sex with a whore.

These conflicing desires understandably generate a tremendous amount of guilt and anxiety in the macho man's mind. Due to the subliminal influence of the Macho Ideal, he unknowingly finds himself looking for two radically different types of women at the same time (which can only rarely be found in the same person). Society, however, tells him that he can only "have" (or be married to) one woman at a time. As a consequence, he typically chooses to marry the "good" girl in his life, and to pursue his *real* sexual desires "on the side." This is perhaps the greatest reason of all why so many men are driven to go out on their wives.

It is also a major reason why so many men hate the members of the opposite sex. Since these masculine individuals can't seem to find everything they want in a single mate, they tend to blame the woman for not being everything a woman should be. Indeed, the very possession of two mutually exclusive desires *itself* tends to arouse a great deal of anger in a man, because it is very disorienting and confusing to want two radically different things at once in the same person. Unfortunately, most macho-oriented men tend to perceive sexual adeptness and personal niceness as being mutually exclusive (though this isn't necessarily the case at all).

These conflicting desires are also responsible for making the macho man feel guilty in some capacity, because he has to neglect his wife (or girlfriend) in order to fulfill his sexual desires. This guilt also tends to be translated into significant amounts of anger and hostility towards the marital partner.

**21**

No one wants to be involved in a no-win situation, least of all the macho man who wants to be able to have his cake and eat it, too. However, as far as he is concerned, there is nothing wrong with wanting to pursue one's inner desires to the maximum, even if it means having two radically different types of women at the same time. *No wonder* the macho man is so hostile and angry most of the time.

Pornography only serves to intensify this hostility response, because it unconsciously conditions the viewer to associate sexiness with sluttiness. This translates into an individual who *expects* a woman to be slutty in order to be sexually attractive. However, when this heightened sexual expectation becomes thwarted in the real world (as it inevitably must be), the frustrated male typically can't help but respond in an angry fashion. From this point of view, pornography is indirectly responsible for generating a tremendous amount of male violence against women, because it promotes a false and destructive attitude towards feminine sexuality.

Fortunately, it is possible for some men to overcome their addiction to slutty sex, but only if they can be made to realize that sexiness isn't necessarily synonymous with sluttiness. This realization can be facilitated if the man is shown how his unconscious belief in the Macho Ideal has contributed to his underlying desire for slutty women. The fact is, a good clean woman CAN be extremely sexy without being slutty, but only if a man's perception of feminine sexuality isn't being polluted by the false dictates of the Macho Ideal.

Men who have thus been freed from their bondage to the Macho Ideal no longer find slutty women attractive at all. To the contrary, they typically find femininity to be sexually attractive in its own right, without having to be perverted into the sick, macho caricature of slutty "love."

### Adultery and the Incest Taboo

There is an even deeper reason why so many males tend to be drawn outside the marital relationship in order to satisfy their sexual desires. It has to do with an unconscious psychological impulse in the human mind known as the *incest taboo*, which as Freud originally pointed out, specifically forbids sex with an immediate family member.

Virtually all cultures have perpetuated some form of the incest taboo, which have as their basic common element the supposition that "you don't have sex with the person you take the trash out with." This impulse has remained in the human collective unconscious for thousands of years, and for good reason: it has been shown to enhance the survivability of the entire human race through a diversification of its cumulative genetic content, which has the effect of making individuals hardier and more resistant to genetic disease.

Getting back to the level of the individual man in society, we find that the incest taboo is perfectly appropriate for a man's own nuclear family, since it forbids sex with one's own mother or sister. It is only when a man unconsciously generalizes this incest taboo over to his wife (who is really a new family member) that he gets into trouble, because the incest taboo only applies to one's own immediate family, *not* to the woman that one has freely chosen to spend the rest of one's life with. Unfortunately, the unconscious portion of a man's mind is often unable to draw such a neat distinction between a man's freely chosen wife and his own nuclear family. This is undoubtedly due to the fact that he has been rigorously conditioned from a very early age to avoid incestuous relations with anyone in his own immediate family. The extent of this conditioning is so pervasive that it tends to generalize itself in a man's adult years to include *anyone* he happens to be living with in a close family relationship, *including his wife.*

The reason for this very destructive form of generalization is a process known as *classical conditioning* in the psychological literature. It takes place when an unconditioned stimulus, such as the sight of food for a dog, is repeatedly paired with a conditioned stimulus, such as the ringing of a bell. At first, only the unconditioned stimulus (food) is able to elicit the unconditioned response, which would be salivation. However, with enough pairings between the sound of a bell and the sight of food, a dog tends to associate the ringing of the bell with the sight of food, so that eventually, the dog will salivate upon the mere perception of a bell ringing.

It is much the same with the incest taboo in humans. The unconditioned stimulus in this case would be forbidden sex with an immediate family member, while the conditioned stimulus would be those relatively mundane qualities that are routinely associated with close family life, such as housecleaning, taking out the trash, and the like. At first, only the unconditioned stimulus is able to elicit the unconditioned response of not wanting to have incestuous relations with anyone in one's own immediate family. However, when this unconditioned stimulus is repeatedly paired with the types of conditioned stimuli mentioned above, these conditioned stimuli are eventually able to elict the same types of reactions that the unconditioned stimuli themselves were originally able to do.

What this means in everyday terms is that a man who has been conditioned his entire life by the incest taboo tends to unconsciously become conditioned into associating the everyday facts of family life with the notion of forbidden sex. As a consequence, when a man gets married and finds himself performing the same sorts of family functions that he originally performed in his own nuclear family, he may eventually experience a marked aversion to the idea of having sex with his wife, not because there is anything wrong with her, but because the conditioned stimuli that originated during his childhood are still capable of eliciting the same unconditioned response of horror at the thought of having sex with an immediate family member.

This subliminal perception explains why so many "decent" men are driven to look outside the home in order to fulfill their sexual desires. It also explains why many philanderers don't tend to feel very guilty about their extramarital sexual binges: as far as they are concerned, they are just doing what they feel compelled to do in order to fulfill their sexual appetite. If anything, the well-meaning philanderer unconsciously feels as though he is actually being *respectful* to his wife, since he is treating her the same way he originally treated his beloved mother (in the sense of not having sex with her). In his mind, then, there's nothing wrong with what he's doing, because he was taught at a very early age to seek sex *outside* the home, not within it.

Unfortunately, it doesn't usually occur to this kind of man that his wife is *not* his mother, again because the family-induced conditioning surrounding the incest taboo is so overwhelmingly strong: not only does it forbid sex with an immediate family member, it also tends to forbid sex with an *acquired* family member as well (at least in this type of susceptible male).

Needless to say, this aversion to intramarital sex almost always has the effect of generating a tremendous amount of tension and conflict in a macho man's mind. It also tends to generate a respectable amount of hostility in his wife's mind as well, and this only serves to exacerbate his overall hostility reaction against her. It is *very* stressful for a man to be both attracted to, and repulsed by, his own wife—so much so, in fact, that he is often driven to alcohol or drug abuse in order to quell his anxiety. No wonder this kind of individual tends to direct so much of his hate and resentment towards his wife. Since she is the primary focus of his emotional ambivalence, he tends to blame *her* for his inner anxiety and heartache, and this in turn tends to have disastrous consequences for both parties.

The resolution of this problem is straightforward but difficult. The afflicted man needs to be brought to realize that the incest taboo is no longer an appropriate source of motivation for him, since he is no longer living with any immediate family members. This means understanding that it's perfectly okay to have sex with the person you take the trash out with, as long as she's *not* a member of your immediate family. It may take a while, though, for this sort of "anti-family conditioning" to set in, especially if a man expects a woman to be a mother to him. Unfortunately, this sort of unconscious conditioning is notoriously hard to treat effectively, because it extends to the very foundations of a man's psyche. Nevertheless, there is good cause for optimism in this area, because conditioned responses *can* be extinguished with the appropriate behavioral therapy, but only if they are treated consistently and aggressively enough by a trained therapist. Consciousness-raising can also help tremendously here as well, because if a man can be brought to understand why he finds his wife so sexually aversive, he may actually be able to overcome this very insidious sexual hangup from the past.

# Polygamy, Dependency, and the
## Biologically-based Role Asymmetries
## Between Men and Women

As Paris-based philosopher Jacqueline Trouveau has so aptly pointed out, Nature herself has presented men and women with two radically different sociological programmes. Since women have been granted the luxury (and burden) of carrying the unborn child and nursing it through infancy, they almost always possess a deeper emotional bond to their children than men do.

The sheer power of this bonding is evidenced by the many surrogate mother cases that have come to court recently. Even when a woman knowingly contracts her body out to a childless couple for a large sum of money, she is often so overwhelmed with love for her baby when it is born that she is typically unable to give it up without suffering extreme emotional duress. The majority of men are probably incapable of forming such a profound emotional bond with their children, since they are only indirectly involved in the genesis of a baby's life. (Of course, this isn't to say that men are incapable of forming deep, lasting bonds with their children. It is only to say that women are typically capable of forming deeper bonds overall with their children than men are, due to their direct participation in the life-giving process.)

With such a greater degree of attachment overall, women tend to find themselves being more committed to their children's health and well-being than men generally are. In order to faithfully serve this commitment, however, most women find that they need to rely on men to help them with the money and physical protection they need to protect their children from the harsh realities of life.

The point is simply that as far as the issue of childrearing is concerned, women tend to need men much more than men need women. Women need men to help them raise their children, but men don't usually experience the same sort of need toward women, since they typically aren't nearly as involved with the raising of their children as mothers are. Again, they haven't had the opportunity to be as biologically connected to their children as women naturally are (via the placenta and the breast), so they are forced to rely primarily on a love-based sense of duty to tie them to their wives and children. This sense of duty, of course, isn't nearly as strong or compelling as the direct physical bonding that usually takes place between mothers and their children.

When the moral and emotional immaturity of the macho male is added to this biologically-based role asymmetry, we find that many such individuals tend to feel little reason to be sexually faithful to their wives and families. This would seem to explain why so many men are unable to control their urge to run around with other women. It would also seem to explain why more men than women have been philanderous in the past. Being physically tied to the process of bearing and raising children, within the overall context of an oppressive patriarchal society, women simply haven't had the opportunity to be as polygamous as men.[14] The extreme volatility of the male sex drive, of course, has only exacerbated this male tendency to be desirous of many sexual partners.

The primary point to be gleaned from this discussion is that a great many men, especially those who believe in the dictates of the Macho Ideal, tend to regard this biologically-based role asymmetry between men and women as a type of nature-given justification for being polygamous. These individuals like to think that it is okay for them to be philanderous, simply because Nature herself has given them the opportunity to be this way. When this conviction (which may be unconscious) is coupled with the privileged status that has been conferred upon men by the Macho Ideal, we find that a huge proportion of men actually *expect* to be able to run around on their wives with little or no harmful repercussions.

A great many societies in the past have allowed this macho-oriented attitude to openly express itself in the sociological mores between men and women. Many ancient Arabic and Hebrew societies, for instance, allowed their men to possess several wives. More recently and closer to home, several Mormon sects have also allowed their men to possess several wives (though this practice is now officially frowned upon). Even in those societies where bigamy is illegal, the possession of multiple mistresses is often surprisingly well-tolerated. This kind of relaxed attitude towards adultery can be found in France, Italy, Spain, and throughout Latin America. Indeed, the shocking fact of the matter is that some form of polygamy is practiced in *twice* as many societies as monogamy.[15]

In America, however, women have liberated themselves to the point that they now find themselves equal to men in terms of many of their basic rights and privileges. Indeed, women now have access to most of the same high-status jobs that once belonged exclusively to men.

One of the most important results of this liberation has been that women in America aren't nearly as tolerant of philanderous behavior as women of other cultures tend to be. Indeed, it is safe to say that the majority of American women would like to see the same standard of behavior applied to *both* sexes as far as the subject of adultery is concerned. According to this equal standard, if women aren't supposed to cheat on their husbands, then husbands aren't supposed to cheat on their wives either; conversely, if it's okay for men to cheat on their wives, then it should also be okay for wives to cheat on their husbands. The widespread adoption of this equal standard in the United States undoubtedly helps to explain why the adultery rate for American women has now almost caught up with the adultery rate for American men.

As a consequence, American women are now confronting the Macho Ideal head-on by standing up to their husbands and demanding marital fidelity. Macho-oriented men, on the other hand, are still expecting to be able to act on their internal philanderous urges with little or no serious consequence, since they subconsciously feel that their superior status as macho males automatically gives them the right to fool around as much as they want.

Needless to say, when this privileged male attitude faces off against an equally resistant feminist response, the stage is set for a serious (and even potentially bloody) confrontation. For as far as the dictates of the Macho Ideal are concerned, it is a heresy of the most serious kind for lowly females to reproach their superior male counterparts, especially when it comes to the touchy subject of "other women."[16] This is why so many macho-oriented males tend to react with open hostility whenever women confront them on this issue: because they cannot tolerate any kind of haughty challenge to their inner code of ethics. Like the religious fanatic who reacts with violent hostility whenever his religion is blasphemed by others, the macho male tends to react with a similar kind of hostility whenever his inner "religion" is blasphemed by female "unbelievers." This hostility, of course, can manifest itself in a wide variety of ways, including profound marital discord, family violence, and divorce.

*Dependency as an Additional Source of Male Resentment*
It is no secret that men tend to be extremely dependent on the important women in their lives. As Herb Goldberg explains, much of this dependency is rooted in infancy and childhood:

As an embryo and fetus he is placenta-dependent. At birth he is breast-dependent, and throughout his early boyhood he is profoundly dependent on his mother as his primary human relationship. *She* is the one who holds, rocks, cleans, comforts, and clothes him. *She* sets his limits, teaches him right from wrong, reinforces him with praise and controls him with punishment. The female child has also been dependent on her mother, a female figure, but has no comparable deep-rooted dependency on the male for her psychic nourishment.[17]

It is in this manner that males are conditioned early on to be extremely dependent on females. Somewhere between puberty and full adulthood, this dependency is unconsciously transferred from mother to girlfriend, and then later, when the male is ready for marriage, it is transferred from girlfriend to wife.

It is important to understand that, despite the goal of emotional independence that has been fostered by the Macho Ideal, most men remain extremely vulnerable to strong feelings of dependency toward women throughout adulthood:

> Despite the bravado and noises he makes about not allowing a woman to control or dominate him in order that he might maintain his fantasy of being stronger and totally in control of the relationship, the male unconsciously comes to see the female as his lifeline—his connection to survival and his energy source. Many adult men, once they have established a primary relationship with a woman, begin to abandon almost all of their other relationships. The dependency becomes increasingly intense and the crisis, if and when she does leave him, is often life-shattering.[18]

It is precisely this dependency that incites the male to much of the hostility he feels toward women, *because it directly contradicts the ethos of the Macho Ideal*. The truly macho man is not supposed to be emotionally or physically dependent on anyone or anything at all, *especially* women. He is dependent only on himself, and he can make it in life entirely on his own.

In reality, though, the modern male finds that he is not even close to measuring up to this ridiculous standard, since he knows that he is vulnerable to the enormous power of the feminine in his life. Whether or not he is actually dependent on a woman in the present is almost beside the point, because he senses that in the right situation, he will become thoroughly dominated by a woman.

**30**

Much of the reason for this vulnerability is that he feels like he needs a woman in his life in order to be happy. In and of itself, of course, there is nothing wrong with this, because we all need each other in order to lead happy and fulfilled lives. The problem with many men, though, is that they often tend to get carried away by extreme feelings of dependency on women. This fear of losing emotional control to a woman generates a tremendous amount of fear in the male psyche, and this in turn motivates the male to set up an internal wall of resistance against the prospect of being dominated in this fashion. He does this because he unconsciously realizes that once his unconscious defense "is penetrated by a woman...," he will become "...profoundly attached to the point of deep and almost total dependency."[19] This fear of emotional vulnerability generates its own unique form of hostility, because it directly contradicts the lofty demands of the Macho Ideal, which he has subconsciously chosen to place on himself.

The point is simply that for the man who tends to equate any sort of emotional dependency on a woman with a serious degree of male inadequacy, being dependent on a female, or even being *potentially* dependent, tends to generate intense feelings of resentment and hostility towards females. These feelings seem to emanate from a type of subconscious *castration anxiety* in the susceptible male, since he is afraid of losing his manhood (and hence his genitals) if he loses control of his life to a woman. It is a frightful thought indeed for the macho-oriented individual to realize that he could easily lose control of his life to a lowly woman, whose function, according to the Macho Ideal, is supposed to be to serve the male in *his* quest for happiness. No wonder this type of man tends to feel so much resentment towards the opposite sex: in reality, he is scared to death of losing his precious independence to them.

### Dependency and the Fear of Death

These dependency fears actually go far beyond the role of women in a man's life. As Ernest Becker showed so well in his Pulitzer Prize-winning book *The Denial of Death*, a man's fear of dependency is ultimately rooted in his unconscious fear of death. According to Becker, virtually all men are inherently terrified of the possibility of self-annihilation, so much so, in fact, that they cannot bear to face this possibility with their conscious minds. Consequently, they tend to repress their existential death fears into their unconscious minds, so they won't have to experience them in a direct fashion.

Interestingly enough, there is a close intra-psychic relationship between a man's dependency fears and his fear of death. Since both of these fears seems to exist on the same existential continuum in the mind, a man's dependency fears can actually serve to reawaken his underlying fear of death. This can happen because death is the ultimate consequence of humanity's lack of full existential independence.

That is to say, there seems to be an existential continuum in the mind that runs from total dependence, on the one extreme, to total independence, on the other. We are inherently dependent creatures because we are definitely *not* totally self-sufficient. If we were, we would be immortal, and thus immune from physical annihilation. But no one is free from the scourge of death, and this includes the macho male. Although we are always striving to become totally independent from potentially hostile outside forces, we can never succeed completely, because we are all doomed to die eventually. Death therefore represents the most extreme form of human dependence.

Going one step further, since we are naturally so terrified of death, anything that serves to remind us of our own eventual demise is bound to stimulate our unconscious death fears. It is for this reason that most forms of human dependence are capable of generating an intense amount of existential anxiety in the mind, since they tend to remind us, if only at an unconscious level, of our own eventual demise.

This fact is doubly troublesome for the macho male, because it directly contradicts the ethos of the Macho Ideal. As you will recall, the Macho Ideal emphasizes strength, prowess, and, most of all, complete independence over all aspects of a man's life. This is why our superhero movies are so enormously popular with most men: the protagonists of these movies (such as Arnold Schwarzenegger and Sylvester Stallone) completely embody all the precepts of the Macho Ideal, and as a consequence, they are predictably victorious over every conceivable type of outside threat. This, of course, is the goal that almost all men are unconsciously striving for, which in turn explains why so many men tend to receive vicarious satisfaction whenever they watch the exploits of their superheros on the silver screen.

Back in the real world, we find that whenever a man is dependent on another human being (especially a woman), he is actually contradicting the spirit and letter of the Macho Ideal, which centers around the goal of absolute independence in a man's life. This contradiction with his unconscious ethical standard causes him a great deal of anger and anxiety, for as we have seen, whenever the specific

**32**

dictates of the Macho Ideal are contradicted in a susceptible man's life, he tends to experience a great deal of anger and hostility. This anger is compounded by the simultaneous reawakening of his unconscious death fears, which, as we have seen, tend to seep into consciousness whenever a man's dependency fears become stimulated.

These factors understandably cause many men to feel immensely uncomfortable at the prospect of being a dependent, contingent being in life. While these dependency fears in and of themselves don't necessarily have anything to do with women directly, men nevertheless tend to want to vent their fears and resentments onto their female partners, who are a convenient target. This anger becomes greatly intensified if the male is overly dependent on his female mate.

Indeed, because a macho man's self-conceived superiority is defined in terms of his relative status toward women, the act of putting a woman down has the effect of bolstering his own self-image, because the lower a woman seems to be on this "hierarchy of intrinsic value," the higher up the man appears to be. This is the reason for much of the intense fighting seen in marital relationships.

According to Susan Forward[20] and Joan Torres, authors of the best-selling book *Men Who Hate Women & The Women Who Love Them*, there is an additional reason why women-hating men (whom they term "misogynists") hack away at the self-esteem of their partners: so they can make themselves less vulnerable to being abandoned. If such an individual is so dependent on his partner that he is terrified of being abandoned, he will naturally want to do everything in his power to ensure that she will never leave him. For many men (especially those of the macho variety), the best way to do this is to hack away at their partner's self-esteem, typically to the point that she is *incapable* of leaving him.

> According to Forward and Torres, we all need to:
> ...feel emotionally taken care of, to be loved, and to feel safe. As adults we fulfill these yearnings through physical intimacy, emotional sharing, and parenting. But the misogynist finds these yearnings terribly frightening. His normal needs to be close to a woman are mixed with fears that she can annihilate him emotionally. He harbors a hidden belief that if he loves a woman, she will then have the power to hurt him, to deprive him, to engulf him, and to abandon him. Once he has invested her with these awesome and mthical powers, she becomes a fearful figure for him.

**33**

In an effort to assuage these fears, the misogynist sets out, usually unconsciously, to make the woman in his life less powerful. He operates from the secret belief that if he can strip her of her self-confidence, she will be as dependent on him as he is on her. By making her weak so that she cannot leave him, he calms some of his own fears of being abandoned.

All these intense, conflicting emotions make the misogynist's partner not only an object of love and passion but the focal point of his rage, his panic, his fears, and inevitably his hatred.[21]

It is for these reasons that women tend to bear the full brunt of the macho male's inability to properly deal with his death and dependency fears. This understandably generates a tremendous amount of anger and resentment on the part of the woman, which in turn only serves to exacerbate the anger felt by the man. This is due to the fact that the woman's rebellion involves a further contradiction with the internal precepts of the Macho Ideal, which, in its strong form, dictates that women should willingly, and even *happily* bear the full brunt of a man's emotional struggles in life. This vicious cycle of anger building upon anger often continues unabated until one or both parties eventually explodes from the pressure and loses control.

The ultimate reason for this male volatility can be traced to the fact that the Macho Ideal of the dependent male is being violated in three separate ways:
1) by his very dependence on another human being, which shows that he is not the totally self-sufficient man that the Macho Ideal says he should be,
2) by fact that he is dependent on a creature whom the Macho Ideal says should be inferior to him, and
3) by the fact that his woman is choosing to rebel against his anger and hostility, which tells him that she is not the "subservient cog in the male machine" that the Macho Ideal says she should be.

### The Sinister Female

In many men's minds, the death and dependency fears noted above tend to be personified together into a single archetypal image: that of the sinister, virulent female. Within this broad stereotype lies the image of a woman who is so powerful that she is capable of completely destroying a man's life and mind.

This archetype of the sinister female has found expression in many different aspects of our popular culture. Rudyard Kipling wrote about it, and it is a theme that can be found in a large number of book and movie plots. The fact is, a sizable proportion of men are convinced that there really are a large number of women out there who are so strong and evil that they will completely annihilate a man if they are given half the chance.

When this belief is viewed from the limited mindset of the macho male, there is a certain ring of truth to it: because of the internal weaknesses that these individuals possess deep inside themselves, they are unable to act from a truly mature and independent position in their lives. As a consequence, women are inadvertently allowed to exercise an undue amount of power and influence over their lives, which in extreme situations can result in unmitigated catastrophe. It would be wrong, though, to entirely blame the females for these tragedies and to label them as sinister, because in most instances they aren't. They simply reflect back on the ignorance and immaturity of their male partner, who was weak enough to allow such a thing to happen in the first place.

The upshot of this observation is that there would be no sinister females in the world if there were no irrational and immature men out there to project this image onto them. While there may be women in the world who actually feel driven to destroy men's lives (perhaps as a way to get back at the males who abused them early in life), these women would be unable to possess any power at all over a man's life if the man were sufficiently mature, independent, and therefore impervious to outside attack.

This process of blaming others for our own mistakes illustrates a powerful intra-psychic principle. It is called *psychic projection*, and it is one of the most important reasons why the idea of the sinister female is able to provoke such intense anger and hostility reactions in the macho male: because deep down he seems to realize that this female virulence is actually a reflection of his *own* internal inadequacy as a man, and it is this realization that reminds him that he is falling far short of the masculine ideal that he has subconsciously chosen to adopt for himself. This realization causes him to project his anger and hostility onto unsuspecting members of the opposite sex.

# The Anatomy of the Male
# Hostility Response

AS WE HAVE SEEN, THE AMOUNT OF HOSTILITY that is experienced in a macho man's life tends to be directly related to the number of times his masculine code of ethics (the Macho Ideal) is contradicted by the various facts of his own personal life. The more often it is contradicted, the more hostility he tends to feel as a result.

There are several important explanations for this sort of response. For one thing, no one wants to have their precious code of ethics challenged and contradicted by the events in their own personal life, least of all the "real" (i.e. macho-oriented) individual. Indeed, it seems to be a general principle of human behavior that people tend to become agitated when their internal ethical standard (which everyone possesses in one form or another) is violated by the data of their real-world experience. In this sense, the macho man is simply reacting in a stereotypical way to the internal ethical standard he was raised to believe in. Since he was taught from a very young age to believe in the unconditional superiority of men at all levels of human society, he feels strongly compelled to react with anger and hostility when the details of his own personal life fall short of this masculine ideal.

There is also a deeper psychological reason for the male hostility response that we have already briefly discussed. It has to do with an avoidance of the *castration anxiety* that tends to surface whenever a man's sense of masculinity is brought into question. As we have seen, macho males tend to derive their masculine identity largely from their internal allegiance to the Macho Ideal. Hence, when this Ideal is openly contradicted in a susceptible man's life, he tends to feel threatened by the potential loss of his masculinity, which is defined in terms of his allegiance to the Macho Ideal. This fear of losing one's manhood is called "castration anxiety" in the psychoanalytic literature, and a macho man will understandably do everything in his power to avoid it, just as he will do everything in his power to protect the integrity of his own genitals (which directly symbolize the very essence of masculinity).

It is this identification of a man's masculinity with the Macho Ideal that is responsible for causing most of the problems associated with male violence and hostility in our society, especially when it comes to women. This is because each time a susceptible male experiences an event that contradicts his internal standard of masculinity, his very identity as a man comes into jeapordy, and he is then forced into making a radical choice: either he can continue to believe in this unconscious code of ethics, and react with hostility, or he can give up this ethical standard altogether, and his masculinity in the process. Since most macho males would rather die than give up their masculinity, the vast majority choose to react with anger and hostility whenever their internal ethical standard is contradicted from without.

### Inferiority and the Male Hostility Response

This description of the etiology of the male hostility response is consistent with the views of psychiatrist Milton Layden, as set forth in his book *Escaping The Hostility Trap.*[22] According to Layden, we all have two basic psychological needs: to feel equal to our peers in our day-to-day lives, and to have this status supported by our daily experiences. However, when we encounter disrespect from others, this tends to make us feel inferior, and this in turn tends to generate a corresponding amount of hostility within us as an automatic part of the mind's own balancing mechanism. No one wants to feel inferior, because it makes us feel worthless and shameful in our psychological lives; if anything, we want to feel *superior* to others. This is why we tend to react with hostility whenever we are disrespected by others: the anger response catapaults us from a feeling of inferiority to one of superiority, which helps to balance out our initial inferiority feelings.

According to Layden, then, we feel hostility toward others in direct proportion to three related factors:

1) the degree of disrespect we receive from them,
2) the extent to which we feel inferior as a result, and
3) the extent to which we feel superior, or *think* we should feel superior.

Layden's conceptualization fits nicely within the psychological paradigm being presented in this book. For as we have seen, the Macho Ideal unconsciously conditions males to believe that they are superior to females in every relevant way. However, since the realities of normal everyday life make it virtually impossible for these masculine goals to realistically be attained, even by the most heroic of men, those males who unconsciously choose to subscribe to the dictates of the Macho Ideal can't help but feel inferior in their innermost selves, since the details of their own personal lives can never measure up to the lofty standards dictated by this unrealistic masculine standard. And since inferior feelings of *any* kind tend to give rise to hostility reactions, the man who measures the value of his life in terms of the Macho Ideal can't help but react with anger and hostility in his day-to-day life, especially towards those individuals whom he believes are most responsible for causing him to feel so inferior (namely women).

## A Case History

Consider, if you will, the case of Jack, a successful stockbroker. Like most men in this country, Jack was raised to believe in the unspoken ethos of the Macho Ideal. As a consequence, he grew up believing that women were supposed to be used as mere tools in the pursuit of male happiness, not to be treated as equals who deserve a maximum amount of respect from men. Here's how Jack described his own position to me:

> I don't know what all the fuss is about. For as long as I can remember, I always recall thinking that women weren't as important in the overall scheme of things as men. I always thought that their primary function in life was to be "barefoot, pregnant, and in the kitchen." I don't know where I learned this idea from, but it seemed to come from everywhere. The old T.V. shows I used to watch, like "Father Knows Best," all seemed to portray the man as being the more important of the two sexes. Since the man was supposed to be more important than the woman, he was also supposed to be more privileged as well. This view was supported in a big way in my own family, since my mother played the traditional "servant" role to my strong and dominant father. She even seemed to like it. Mom did anything and everything my father ever asked of her.
>
> In addition, whenever I looked out onto the scientific and political scene, I saw that virtually all of the significant figures throughout history have been males. It's not hard to see why: we're bigger and stronger than women are, and for the most part, we're smarter too.

As I listened to Jack describe his attitude toward women, it was easy to see why women have accumulated so much anger and resentment toward men over the years. At the same time, though, his underlying attitude toward the opposite sex was clearly so ridiculous that it was difficult to take seriously. It is hard to believe that people still think such outrageously inaccurate thoughts about themselves. Indeed, perhaps this is one reason why women have been so tolerant of macho behavior over the years: it's so ridiculous and even pitiful that it's easy to feel sorry for those individuals who actively display it. What could be worse than thinking and acting like a brutish moron, especially when one thinks the total opposite? In this sense, the overly macho individual is his own worst punishment, since he has unknowingly condemned himself to repeated bouts of public embarrassment, via his compulsively obnoxious and disgusting behavior.

When I asked Jack what made him most angry about women, his answer was so typical that it was almost predictable:

What I hate most about women, especially those "women's libbers," is when they refuse to treat me like a man. You know what I mean: a *real* man. I mean, when they try to take my job away, when they try to take away my right to go out with my buddies, or whatever, I can't help but get mad. All I want to do in my life is be a real man; not a wimp or a sissy like so many women seem to want these days. Is that asking too much? But then, when I see so many hoardes of bitches standing gallantly in my way, I lose my cool. If this is what the future is gonna be like, I belong in the *past*.

At this point, I asked Jack to tell me the worst thing that he had ever done to a woman. His reply didn't surprise me (although it was still quite shocking):

One time, a few years ago, I was dating this broad named Angie pretty seriously. We were even talking about gettin' married. At first, she kissed up to me pretty good, and I thought that I had finally found a real woman to be the mother of my kids. She cleaned my apartment for me, cooked for me, and was just plain good to me. But then, somethin' happened. She must've fallen into the hands of one of those women's libbers and gotten perverted. She quit treatin' me like a man. She started complainin' about my "chauvinistic" attitude and started gettin' real sassy with me. So I decided to show her who was boss. I went out with another broad right in front of everyone; not because I was in love with the cheesy new bitch, but just to put my old lady in her place. When I told her I'd quit goin' out on her if she'd quit bein' so mean to me, she told me to go screw myself. That *really* caused me to flip my lid. So, I slapped the bitch pretty good, but then she tried to do somethin' stupid like

**40**

kick me in the nuts. So I beat the shit outa her. I don't know what came over me. I probably over-reacted, but I couldn't help myself. She should've known better.

It's a sad, but true, sign of the times that Jack's behavior—contemptible though it may be—is *typical* of the way millions of men feel toward women. In fact, over three million cases of wife-battering[23] take place each and every year, but only a small minority of these incidents actually get reported to the police. In fact, a woman is much more likely to get assaulted, raped or beaten by a male partner than by a stranger.[24] Figures like these demand that we take a serious look into the origins of the male hostility response toward women, so that it can be dealt with in an appropriate way and hopefully resolved. It's clear that Jack's hostility toward Angie was initiated when the specific details of his personal life began to fall seriously short of the dictates specified by the Macho Ideal. As soon as Angie quit treating him like some sort of macho god, Jack saw that wouldn't be able to live up to the high standard of behavior that he had unknowingly set up for himself, at least not with Angie. This is why he lost control of his behavior when she told him to get lost: because it told him in no uncertain terms that he was not in total control of his life, as the Macho Ideal says he should have been.

The point to be gleaned from this discussion is simply that when the disparity between personal reality and the Macho Ideal becomes too great, the susceptible male can't help but become hostile.

### Discussion: Religion and the Macho Ideal

It is hard to convey the vast importance of the Macho Ideal in most men's lives. Since it helps to constitute their innermost identity as "true men," it is the most important thing in the world to them. This explains why they are so incredibly devoted to it on a deep, subconscious level. This level of belief is so intense that it can be properly described as being "religious." After all, a religion is simply a belief in something larger than oneself that helps to give one's life structure and meaning. This describes the Macho Ideal perfectly.

The Macho Ideal also contains within itself the ethical specifications for "correct" or "good" masculine behavior. This organizing of a man's life is unconsciously perceived like a god, since it represents the very lifeblood of all meaningful actions in the world. No wonder macho men tend to get so enraged when the dictates of the

Macho Ideal are openly challenged or contradicted by anyone or anything in their lives. With a fervor that can only be described as "religious," such a challenge typically brings forth the full wrath of the devout person whose religion has been desecrated and humiliated by heathen unbelievers. One has only to look at the incredible number of crimes against humanity that have been faithfully carried out by members of a wide variety of different religious organizations to see how much anger can be generated in a devout person whose religion is openly flouted.

The "true believer" in the Macho Ideal behaves in much the same way when his inner masculine standard is violated by a woman. He tends to feel so threatened that he often acts as though his very own mother has been attacked, so he tends to become violently enraged. In his own mind, this extreme anger is perfectly justified, because he is simply responding to a perceived threat to the underlying meaning of his entire life (which constitutes his true religion). This is why he often gets violently angry whenever his inner sense of masculinity is openly attacked by a woman: because he feels like his very identity as a man is being threatened, and this is something he is willing to fight to the death to protect. It doesn't matter that this masculine standard is totally in error, because as far as he is concerned, it is the most important thing in his entire life. It follows, then, that as long as he insists on serving his hidden god, he will always be vulnerable to extreme bouts of anger and hostility.

### Homosexuality and the Macho Ideal

Although no controlled studies have been done attempting to relate the incidence of violence and hostility in gay men to their degree of allegiance (or lack thereof) to the Macho Ideal, one would think that a strong direct relationship probably exists here. For one thing, it almost goes without saying that gay men tend to be less hostile and violence-prone on the whole than their straight counterparts; they also seem to be far less subservient to the dictates of the Macho Ideal. While it is possible that this relationship is purely accidental, most people would agree that there is probably a strong causal relationship at work here.

In other words, it doesn't seem to be an accident that gay men tend to be relatively non-hostile and that they also tend to shun society's ideal of a maximum degree of machismo for men. Moreover, it doesn't seem to be an accident that most gay men tend to be a good deal more pleasant and easy to get along with than their straight counterparts.

(The airlines have been aware of this fact for a long time, since the vast majority of male flight attendants, who need to be as pleasant as possible, seem to be gay.) As we all know, it is very difficult indeed to be pleasant to others when one is full of anger and hostility deep inside. It would seem to follow, then, that the less angry and hostile one is on the inside, the more pleasant one is likely to be on the outside. But it is precisely the Macho Ideal that tends to make most men angry; hence, the less one subscribes to the dictates of the Macho Ideal, the less likely it is that one will be inordinately hostile in one's day-to-day life, and the more likely it is that one will outwardly be more pleasant and easy to get along with.

This also explains why most macho men appear to be so dry, smug, and even "pissed-off" on the whole: because they are profoundly angry deep inside. They are angry, of course, because they are trying to live up to a mythical standard of excellence that can *never* be attained, no matter how hard they may try.

It is very difficult to be happy when one is striving for a goal that is intrinsically impossible to attain. It is even more difficult to be happy when one bases one's very identity as a man on the attainment of such an impossible goal. No wonder so many macho men are chronically angry and stern-faced: they're ruining their entire lives by chasing after a goal that is intrinsically impossible to obtain.

The resolution of this problem is almost as easy as its identification. For just as soon as the macho individual realizes the absolute ludicrousness of his macho-oriented goal, he can then abandon it forever in favor of a more reasonable objective in life. Happily, once the Macho Ideal itself is abandoned, all the anger and hostility that used to be associated with it will spontaneously disappear as well.

**43**

# Male Hostility and the
# Working Woman

ANOTHER TRIGGER OF THE MALE HOSTILITY RESPONSE is rooted in the increasing stature of women in the work force. In the past, when the ethos of the Macho Ideal was more firmly entrenched in the structure of American society, men were the ones who were expected to work, especially in such important fields as law and medicine, while women were expected to stay home and raise the children. To this day, many men (and women) *still* think that the proper role for a woman in society is to be "pregnant, barefoot, and in the kitchen."

The reason for this ridiculous expectation is once again to be found in the unspoken credo of the Macho Ideal. If men really are as important and superior as the Macho Ideal says they should be, then it is only natural that they should occupy the most important roles in society, while women should be relegated to the more subservient, background-type roles. Moreover, since men require a stable and functional home base in order to be able to function efficiently in society, and since a traditional "housewife" is an important part of this home economy, the Macho Ideal dictates that women should willingly take on this subservient role for themselves. This specification is further reinforced by the fact that women are traditionally the ones who are most capable of caring for the young.

Today, however, things are vastly different. Instead of barely being represented in the medical, legal, and business communities, as was true in the past, women are now equally represented in many important fields. In fact, there are many areas of employment where women are now considered to be more desirable than men, due to their unique interpersonal and cooperative skills.

The upshot of this relatively recent sociological phenomenon is that the macho male's inner code of ethics is being violated on yet another level. This in turn leads to the development of still *more* male hostility toward women. As Phil exclaimed to me one day, "How dare they come into the work force and compete with me for my job when they are supposed to be taking care of business on the homefront. Not only do I have a wife and kids to support, I think that men are much better qualified for most of the upper-level jobs in society that are now being taken more and more by women."

## Male Hostility and Female Rebelliousness
Part and parcel with the full-scale entry of women into the

workforce has been an increased tendency for women to stand up to the macho antics of men. This in turn greatly angers the macho-oriented individual, because it means that his underlying code of ethics is being contradicted on still another level.

We have seen how the Macho Ideal dictates that the proper role for women in human society is to function as selfless servants for men. If a man sincerely believes this, then he is naturally going to feel a tremendous amount of anger and hostility when a woman refuses to take this kind of subservient, self-negating role in his life. As Jim once declared to me about his now-estranged wife:

> "I knew exactly what I needed from Nina in order to be happy, but she had the audacity to refuse to cooperate with me. She even had the guts to spit back in my face one night when I lost my temper with her! How dare she do that to me! It makes me want to cut her throat sometimes."

Guys like Jim rarely see how *they* are the ones who are guilty of antagonizing their wives into a full-scale rebellion. They find it hard to believe that *they* could be the ones who are pushing their wives over the edge. They simply believe that it is the proper role of a woman to be subservient to her husband through all manner of trial and tribulation, no matter what. They don't realize that such a belief is totally demeaning to a woman. In fact, they believe the opposite: that this kind of female subservience is actually *good* for women! Such is the power of the "poisonous pedagogy" that *is* the Macho Ideal.


### Cultural Reinforcement for the Male Hostility Response

Not only does our patriarchal society help to initiate the male hostility response toward women (through its undue emphasis on the Macho Ideal), it also helps to perpetuate it through the cultural sanctioning of aggressive male behaviors toward women.

> In literature, movies, and television, women are used by men as shields, foils, and hostages. They are raped, beaten, and shot with frightening regularity. Pornography implies that a woman's inherent seductiveness justifies any sadistic and/or sexual act a man wishes to commit against her.

For the misogynist [woman-hater], who comes into adulthood fearful of women and of his strong feelings about them, these cultural messages seem to give him further license to behave cruelly. A culture that has depicted women, from the Bible on, as evil, malignant, and sinister, gives misogynists even more reasons to hate, fear, and revile women.[25]

Although this cultural sanctioning of the male hostility response toward women is to be expected of a pathological, deeply-engrained patriarchal society, it cannot (and should not) be tolerated any more, because of the enormous amount of pain and suffering that is generated daily by it. Too many people are suffering too much pain to ever justify its continued existence.

### Evil and the Macho Ideal

The behavioral control that is exacted upon men by the Macho Ideal qualifies as a genuine, demonic evil in our society. It is a demonic evil because it silently and insidiously possesses a man's mind and compels him to commit evil, destructive acts, oftentimes against his better judgment. It doesn't matter that this sort of "demon possession" emanates from a person's own mind instead of from an external spiritual agent, because this inner evil can always be personified in the form of a spiritual devil.

This characterization of the Macho Ideal in terms of demonic evil is not exaggerated at all, because the vast majority of all evil acts that have ever been committed by men can be traced back to this inner pathological force. Moreover, just as the spiritual devil in the Bible must be heroically resisted before he will consent to leave a person alone, the inner evil of the Macho Ideal must also be heroically resisted by the light of consciousness before it will disappear once and for all.

# Unconscious Sources of Hostility

A MAJOR SOURCE OF HOSTILITY IN HUMAN LIFE has nothing directly to do with the Macho Ideal, or even with present-day events as such. This source of hostility resides within the unconscious mind, and it has its origin in the emotional conflicts that we all experienced during childhood.

Sigmund Freud was the first major thinker to realize that the human mind has a strong unconscious component to it. Freud believed that the ego protects itself from its worst pains and fears by locking them away inside the unconscious as a psychological means of defense. C.G. Jung—who began his study of the unconscious with Freud but eventually branched out on his own—built on this fundamental notion and eventually came out with his own brand of analytic psychology that emphasized the intrinsic gender differences between the sexes. However, it wasn't until the ground-breaking work of Arthur Janov in the early 1970's that the role of the unconscious in human life became fully incorporated into a comprehensive therapeutic scheme that actually worked. Janov's publication of *The Primal Scream* in 1970 revolutionized our understanding of the unconscious, and in the process, it finally gave us a tool for understanding many of the problems that have plagued interpersonal relationships for millennia.

In this chapter we will explore the two major sources of hostility that emanate from within the unconscious itself: Jung's concept of the *anima* and Janov's concept of *Primal Pain*.

### The Anima

Jung believed that all psychic traits naturally exist in the mind as antinomies; that is, in conjunction with their logical opposites. As far as the psychic characteristic of masculinity is concerned, this means that a man also has a feminine aspect to his unconscious, which Jung termed the *anima*. Women have a corresponding masculine component to their psyches as well, which Jung termed the *animus*.

In other words, "the psychological facts indicate that every human being is androgenous,"[26] or comprised of both masculine and feminine psychological characteristics. The Russian philosopher Nicholas Berdyaev agrees:

Man is not only a sexual but a bisexual being, combining the masculine and feminine principle in himself in different proportions and often in severe conflict. A man in whom the feminine principle was completely absent would be an abstract being, completely severed from the cosmic element. A woman in whom the masculine principle was completely absent would not be a personality...It is only the union of these two principles that constitutes a complete human being. Their union is realized in every man and every woman within their bisexual, androgenous nature, and it also takes place through the intercommunion between the two natures, the masculine and the feminine.[27]

Jung further believed that these masculine and feminine traits must be expressed in relative balance with one another if psychological health is to be maintained. This means that a man cannot repress his anima—or his feminine side—and expect to "get by" unscathed. Indeed, because of the anima's immense power over the entire male psyche, repressing the anima can have truly devastating consequences in a man's life.

Unfortunately, the very essence of the Macho Ideal is to be found in its complete rejection of everything that is feminine in the male personality. It follows from this proposition that in order to be a "real man," the macho individual must reject all aspects of the feminine in his life. Thus, a global repression of the anima appears to be a *necessary precondition* for the attainment of true masculinity, at least as far as the Macho Ideal is concerned.

The anima, however, doesn't give in without a fight. It continually struggles to reassert itself in the male psyche, because it is an essential feature of the normal human personality. A healthy relationship with one's anima is also a necessary precondition for the attainment of *individuation*, which, according to Jung, represents our species-based goal of self-maturation.

Needless to say, it is exceedingly difficult for the macho-oriented male to come to terms with his own anima, because he is deriving his very identity as a "real man" from its rejection. This is why most men find acceptance of the anima:

...almost invariably difficult. The anima, as Jung points out, is the root word in animosity, and anima (as moods) can be another name for resentment. Initiation by the anima means submitting to painful experiences of betrayal and disappointment when the projections she creates with her capacity for illusion fail to produce happiness. Accepting the pain of one's affects towards those experiences is a critical part of integrating the anima. Jung sometimes called the anima the "archetype of life," and he saw the individual as forced to suffer at the hands of life until life's power is sufficiently impressed upon him: the resultant conscious attitude, truly "a pearl of great price," is a sense of soul, which is also a respect for life's autonomy...[28]

Since the anima refuses to be repressed into the background without a fight, it continually searches for new ways to reassert itself in the male psyche. More often than not, this reassertion ends up wreaking all sorts of havoc in a man's life.

Indeed, due to the cyclical nature of anima-induced suffering, this self-driven destructiveness tends to build on itself in the following manner: The suffering that is initially produced by the anima naturally causes a man to experience an additional amount of pain and misery in his life, which in turn stimulates him to further repress his anima. The anima responds to this additional repression by struggling to reassert itself in an even stronger fashion, which then has the effect of producing still *more* pain and heartache in his life, and so on. This process of self-created frustration and disappointment continues on in a vicious cycle until the man either becomes physically violent as a result or succumbs to some sort of psychosomatic illness.

Teleologically speaking, at least, this isn't a bad state of affairs at all, because people never seem to learn their lessons in life unless they are first made to suffer for a time. Indeed, acceptance of the anima is still immensely difficult for most men, even though they are forced to suffer at its hands on an almost daily basis. It follows, then, that if a man's species-based goal of individuation is to ever be attained, he must continue to suffer indefinitely until he eventually learns his lesson and comes to terms with his own anima.

Clearly, the anima is an exceedingly powerful part of the male psyche that can be tampered with only at one's own peril. However, as long as a man professes belief in the Macho Ideal, he must inevitably be opposed to his own anima, because this is the very essence of male machismo, as we have seen. This is why macho men tend to become so angry and violent in their day-to-day lives: because they are trying to murder an important part of themselves that simply will not go away.

Fortunately, when the dictates of the Macho Ideal are consciously recanted, a man no longer feels prevented from facing the contents of his own anima. Indeed, when such a tacit acceptance of the anima is openly acted upon, he will eventually find that he can live in relative peace with her. At this point the anima's destructive influence upon his life will automatically cease. Having performed its teleological function in reuniting the formerly disparate elements of his masculine psyche, the anima's destructive influence upon his life will spontaneously disappear altogether, leaving behind a much healthier and happier person in its wake.

### The Ultimate Task of True Masculinity

According to the Macho Ideal, the ultimate task of true masculinity is for a man to attain heroic self-mastery, *not* through a legitimate confrontation with the major problems of his life, but through a flaunting denial of their existence and power over him. This is clearly a pathological method of personal problem-solving that is bound to end in tragedy and failure sooner or later. One simply cannot expect to solve the problems in one's life by ignoring them and hoping that they'll go away.

The ultimate task for the anima, on the other hand, is for a man to be capable of empathic participation in life.[29] This process of empathic participation, however, does not exclude the masculine goal of self-mastery. To the contrary, it eventually leads to it, because empathic participation is the only legitimate means of problem-solving in life. For by empathically participating in all aspects of one's day-to-day experience in the world, one naturally confronts one's many problems in a realistic way, so that eventually, with enough patience and hard work, they can be resolved once and for all.

The Macho Ideal, on the other hand, specifically forbids a man to even admit that he has any problems in his life that are in need of resolution. It also forbids him to participate in an empathic fashion in his daily behavior, because such empathic responses threaten to bring him too close to the unconscious feelings that he is trying to avoid.

It follows from these observations that as long as a man continues to pledge allegiance to the Macho Ideal, he will never be able to attain his ultimate male-oriented goal of self-mastery in life. This is one of the greatest ironies in a macho man's life, because in the very act of trying to be a "real man," he ends up blocking his own progress towards this most important of goals (at least until he changes).

### The Role of Primal Pain in the
### Genesis of the Male Hostility Response

Now it is time to turn our attention to Arthur Janov's rendition of the male hostility response. As Janov has pointed out, the most pervasive need in childhood, apart from strictly physiological needs, is for parental love and approval.

Children of all ages crave parental love for two reasons. To begin with, some degree of parental caretaking—which is the most basic form of love—is absolutely essential in the first few months and years of life, because without it the young child cannot survive. Since young children are so profoundly dependent on others for food, warmth, and shelter, they are largely at the mercy of the adult caretakers in their lives. And since love of some form must first exist before a child's caretakers will feel motivated to deliver this precious life-giving care, it follows that a child must be loved in some way in order to survive.

Once the child grows through this initial stage of absolute dependence, however, he or she still requires parental love in order to psychologically develop in a healthy fashion. This need persists throughout childhood and adolescence, and often continues unabated throughout the whole of life (where it is often transferred to other people besides our parents).

According to Janov, this need for love is so strong in young children that any significant privation in this area can help to set the stage for the later development of neurosis. This is why love must be unconditional in order to be effective in preventing neurosis: because as soon as the young child learns that the "love" he receives from his parents is contingent on his performing a required set of behaviors, he quickly comes to the realization that he is not being loved for *who* he really is, but rather, for what he can *do* for his parents.

This realization causes an unbearable amount of pain in the defenseless child's mind. In fact, this lack of unconditional love typically causes the young child so much pain that he is almost always forced to resort to the psychological defense mechanism known as *repression* in order to protect himself from this horrible onslaught of pain. Repression functions to automatically relegate painful feelings to the realm of the unconscious, where they won't have to be directly experienced by the conscious mind.

It is important to understand that this process of repression is an instinctual *survival mechanism* that has served humankind well during its long evolution. Because children are too young to have developed an

**53**

effective means of protecting themselves from emotional pain, they aren't strong enough to be able to face the emotional pain of rejection head-on. Without some way of protecting their fragile egos, then, these youngsters run the risk of catastrophic emotional and physical disintegration.[30]

It would be a mistake, however, to assume that the young child must experience an overwhelming emotional insult in order to be damaged in this manner. Due to the utter fragility of their little egos, along with their lack of adequate psychological defenses, even the tiniest emotional insult can have an extremely catastrophic effect on the growing child's mind.

It is for this reason that the Powers That Be have given us the psychological defense mechanism of repression, so that we can protect ourselves from the inevitable emotional pains of infancy and childhood. Without it, the child's virgin mind is likely to be overwhelmed by the intense emotional harshness of life, often to the point of complete emotional and physical disintegration. In fact, some authors have gone so far as to claim that crib death (Sudden Infant Death Syndrome)—for which no clear etiology has yet been ascertained—actually represents a comprehensive failure of the infant's capacity to contain his repressions. On this view, the sudden flood of repressed pains into the infant's virgin consciousness, some of which may have originated during the actual birth process itself, acts to overwhelm the brain's capacity for coherent self-maintenance. As part of this cognitive disintegration, the brain suddenly loses its capacity to maintain the life function, and death quickly ensues.

Unfortunately, the child's mind remains exquisitely sensitive to parentally-derived emotional pains throughout childhood and adolescence. Even though the child's immediate physical survival may no longer be an issue once he reaches a certain age, his emotional well-being remains *tremendously* sensitive to even the slightest insults from his parents; that is, unless he has already become too defended to notice them. Indeed, this appears to be one of the chief functions of autism and other serious psychological disturbances in some children's minds: to protect them from the tremendous amount of emotional pain in their lives.[31]

We mustn't forget how fragile the child's self-image actually is at this early stage in her psychological development. After all, she is in the very tenuous position of having to create her own self-identity through her own thoughts and actions in the world, and this is probably the most difficult task in all of human development. It follows, then, that prior to full psychological adulthood, the child's final personality structure isn't "all there" yet. This lack of a fully-assembled identity understandably causes her to be exquisitely sensitive to even the slightest intimation that she might not be a truly good and worthwhile person in her own right.

It must be continually borne in mind that young children have absolutely no idea about what they're actually like in the real world. They rely on us to tell them, both through our direct comments to them, as well as through our specific actions in their immediate company. They use feedback from us to help them construct their all-important self-image; this is why what we say and do around them is so utterly important.

Going one step further, we can say that all young children want to be good and worthwhile people, not only for the sake of being quality individuals, but also for the sake of being lovable. Love is by far the single most important commodity to a growing child, as we have seen, because it is necessary to ensure that the child develops in a healthy fashion. Therefore, to the extent that love is lacking in a young child's life, she will be unhappy, because she will find herself being forced to grow in an aversive, pathological manner.

Love is also tremendously reinforcing in and of itself, apart from any growth-facilitating role it may play in the young child's life. Indeed, love is so important to our fragile egos that it remains the most important thing to us throughout our entire adult lives. The finer parts of life simply don't reveal themselves to us *until* and *unless* we are first loved by someone else. It's as if love were an intangible ticket to the most enjoyable show in town.

Given the overwhelming importance of love in the young child's life, along with the tremendous fragility of the child's ego structure, it is no surprise that the lack of love to any significant degree has truly catastrophic effects on the growing child's physical and mental health. An unloving remark or action on the part of an adult (especially a parent) can cause the child to experience a devastating amount of emotional pain. So aversive is this subjective experience of pain that the child will instinctively repress it into his unconscious whenever it exceeds a certain minimum level of intensity. All children do this to some extent, because it is impossible for any parent, no matter how well-intentioned, to offer a perfectly pain-free environment for child-rearing. Some children, however, are forced to repress pain far more frequently than others, due to their own inner sensitivity and the amount of pain they are forced to contend with on a daily basis.

Once the process of repression proceeds beyond a certain minimum point, the child's unconscious "pool" of pain eventually becomes too imposing to be handled innocuously. The mind's repressive capacity becomes overtaxed, and the conscious mind subsequently becomes distorted into the psychopathology of neurosis. Just as heating a sealed teapot that is full of water naturally causes it to be distended at its weakest point, repeatedly pressuring the mind's repressive lid with too many repressions eventually causes the conscious mind to become distorted at *its* weakest point. For some people, this inordinate pressure tends to cause only psychological symptoms, such as anxiety, depression, and overt hostility. For others, the pressure becomes so intense that it automatically spills over into the body, where it can cause facial tics, colitis, and even cancer.

Once the young child has been forced to repress himself into the psychopathology of neurosis, he unconsciously vows to do everything in his power to win the struggle that caused him to repress himself in the first place. This is because the struggle for love is an all-consuming process that tends to dominate a person's entire life, even throughout adulthood.

To illustrate, let us consider the case of a young child who is continually ignored by his mother, no matter what he says or does. This understandably causes the child a tremendous amount of emotional discomfort, since it makes him feel unloved, unimportant, and worst of all, unlovable. The reason for this feeling of rejection, of course, is that it represents the loss of that which is most important to him: his mother's precious love. Consequently, like the dog who has lost his beloved bone and then proceeds to devote his entire life to finding it again, the child who feels that he has lost his mother's love proceeds to devote the rest of his life (albeit unconsciously) to regaining this love.

Nine times out of ten the young child blames himself for his apparent unlovability, because he can't imagine that the real fault actually lies with his parents. When this occurs, the child usually tries to fix the problem by forcing himself to become as good and lovable as possible. If, for instance, he grew up believing that he was not lovable because he had nothing important to say (because one or both parents never took the time to listen to him), then he might eventually become obsessed with becoming an "authority" in a certain area of life, since authorities are typically recognized as having something important to say. The true source of this motivation, however, would probably not be apparent to him, because it would be largely unconscious in nature.

It doesn't occur to young children, or even to most emotionally-scarred adults, that their own parents could have been *wrong* in how they chose to raise their children. This is because most children tend to see their parents as all-knowing and all-powerful, which means that as far as the kids themselves are concerned, anything their parents say or do *must* be right. It follows, then, that if a child's parents seem to think that he or she is bad or unlovable for whatever reason, the child will tend to take them at their word and grow up with a poor self-image.

As long as parents insist on offering conditional love to their children, kids will be forced into struggling to do whatever is necessary to obtain their parent's love. They can't help but get involved in the struggle, because they don't know any better. They simply assume that the struggle must be appropriate, given their profound need for their parents' love and their parents' extreme power and authority over them.

Unfortunately, it often turns out to be the case that the more a child struggles to obtain his parents' love, the less available that love tends to be. This is due to the fact that a struggling child tends to get on his parents' nerves, thereby making them more uncooperative than they were initially. But even if the child succeeds with his struggle by doing whatever is necessary to procure his parents' love, it rarely turns out to be sufficient, *because love that must be struggled for isn't true love at all.* The struggling child, however, is incapable of realizing the futility of his goal; he simply sees his disappointment as proof that he didn't struggle hard enough to obtain his goal. This of course tends to keep the child enmeshed in this type of struggle *indefinitely.*

It is important to understand that winning the struggle for his parents' love is by far the most important thing in the young child's life. Toys, vacations, sweets, and all the other joys of childhood literally pale in comparison to this ever-present goal. Significantly, though, as long as we remain neurotic in our own adult lives, we never outgrow this potent childhood desire. While we may no longer actively struggle with our parents for this love (because it is usually no longer appropriate), the desire to have this primal conflict resolved and fulfilled remains with us throughout our adult lives. We simply transfer the struggle to a more appropriate target: a romantic partner.

This recreation of one's past parental conflict in the present is called a *repetition compulsion.* A repetition compulsion is simply the unconscious urge to recreate, in the present, situations of past conflict, so that a symbolic solution can hopefully be attained. In situations involving past conflict with one or both parents, we tend to find ourselves being romantically attracted to people who resemble in some significant way the parent with whom we had the most conflict. The "purpose" of this kind of sublimated attraction is so we can continue our childhood struggle in the present, which we can only do with individuals who possess the same psychological quality that one or both parents used against us as children.

Unfortunately, this symbolic process of conflict resolution tends to generate its own present-day series of conflicts, which can quickly lead to overt hostility reactions in both sexes (especially in the male, since he is particularly ill-at-ease with his own emotions). It is also hopelessly doomed to failure as well, because symbolic resolutions of past conflicts can never erase the unconscious pain that is associated with them.

Although not everyone seeks to unconsciously resolve their past parental conflicts with a romantic partner in the present, the vast majority of neurotic individuals clearly try to do so. In fact, the more neurotic one is, the more likely one is to seek out a symbolic resolution to one's past conflicts, and the more intense one's attempt is likely to be. This is because neurotics are the ones who are burdened with these unconscious conflicts to begin with. They are also the ones who prefer symbolic resolutions to real-world resolutions, because real-world resolutions require the neurotic to face his unconscious conflicts head-on, and he is typically loathe to do that. The name of the neurotic game, as Janov has pointed out, is the *avoidance* of psychological pain, so the neurotic has little choice but to try to resolve his unconscious conflicts symbolically, via a carefully chosen romantic partner in the present. This, however, constitutes the very essence of neurotic misery, because the neurotic is perpetually trying to solve a problem that can never be solved in this manner.

### *The Mystery of Romantic Love*

As I attempted to show in my earlier book *Why Men Cheat*, much of the mystery surrounding romantic love seems to revolve around this very type of neurotic enmeshment between two people. Even the type of interpersonal "chemistry" that determines whom we fall in love with seems to revolve, at least for those who are sufficiently predisposed, around the unconscious replaying of past parental conflicts in the present. The goal in this type of neurotic enmeshment is simply the attainment of some degree of symbolic satisfaction with one's present-day parent substitute.

In order for this to be accomplished, however, the most important ingredients in one's original parental conflict must be recreated as closely as possible. Otherwise, the resemblance to the past won't be sufficient to elicit the appropriate struggling response, nor will it be sufficient to promise an appropriate symbolic fulfillment.

By far the most important element in the re-creation of this past parental scenario is the psychological profile of the romantic partner. Before an individual can be considered to be an appropriate partner for this type of symbolic fulfillment, he or she must "fit into" the re-creation of this past conflict in some important way. The only way this can be done is if he or she happens to resemble, in some relevant capacity, the parent with whom one had the most conflict. This resemblance doesn't have to be blatant, however. It need only concern the type of attitude or personality trait that caused us to struggle with our parents in the first place.

Interestingly enough, many neurotic individuals seem to have a subconscious radar for the detection of appropriate romantic partners. These individuals seem to have their parents' basic traits imprinted upon their subconscious minds, so that when they finally run into someone in the present who happens to share these same basic character traits, they tend to experience an *immediate* bonding response to them. They feel bonded to them because they are using the same psychic "channels" in their minds that their parents originally utilized.

Many people describe this immediate psychic response as "love at first sight," and in a way, it is. We love these people instantly because they are simply present-day substitutes for our parents, whom we have loved intensely from the start. Clearly, though, it is impossible to truly love another person for who *they* really are at first sight, because one simply hasn't had the chance to get to know them yet. It *is*, however, quite possible for a person to instantly fall in love with someone because they resemble in some important way the parent with whom we had the most conflict. We fall in love in this manner because the psychic channels for this loving response were actually established decades ago by our parents. We "fall" into them again when someone with whom we interact in the present is sufficiently similar to one of our parents to cause us to engage in the same type of emotional response to them. We mustn't forget that we are intimately familiar (albeit on an unconscious level) with those types of parental qualities that we originally struggled with as children; all we need to do to "fall in love" in the present is to find someone who shares these important qualities in a way we find appealing.[32]

The fact that some people can fall in love instantly is a lasting testimony to the power of the unconscious in determining what we are ultimately attracted to in life, and what we are not, especially when it comes to romantic partners. The unconscious can obviously determine, in a mere moment's notice, whether or not we are attracted to a potential partner, and whether or not this person can possibly fit in with our own psychological traits and needs.

This process of interpersonal interaction with a potential romantic partner is called "chemistry," and it seems to be just as automatic and pervasive as physical chemistry can be. For instance, when a hydrogen atom "meets" an oxygen atom, it doesn't have to get to "know" it before it decides whether or not it can bond with it. It instantly "knows," because of the structural configuration of both atoms. Similarly, when two people with the "right" psychological configurations hook up with one another, a romantic "reaction" tends to instantly result, due to the favorable chemistry that naturally exists between them.

### A Brief Note on Spontaneous Reactivity in Interpersonal Relationships

In one important sense, then, people tend to resemble the atoms and molecules of which they are made. As we noted above, atoms and molecules are known to spontaneously combine with those substances with which they have the most chemical affinity. The stronger the chemical attraction, the more likely it is that a given reaction will occur between two chemical species. It doesn't matter that the substance in question may already be "involved" in a previous chemical "relationship"; if another substance comes along whose inherent power of attraction exceeds that of the existing molecular co-factor, it will cause the existing chemical "relationship" to spontaneously "break up," so that it can then form a tighter bond with the new substance.

Opiate antagonists work in very much the same fashion. Opiates such as heroin and morphine are known to bind strongly to opiate receptors in the brain. This is what enables them to exert their powerful pharmocological effects on the mind and body. However, other substances, known as opiate antagonists (such as Nalorphine), are known to form a much stronger bond with the brain's opiate receptors than regular opiates do. This bonding is so strong, in fact, that opiate antagonists can actually force heroin or morphine *out* of the brain's opiate receptors, so that the antagonists themselves can take their place. This is known in pharmocological circles as *competitive inhibition*, and it is what causes the heroin addict to go into spontaneous withdrawal when he is given an injection of Nalorphine.

Human interpersonal relationships are much the same way. People are naturally attracted to one another in a wide variety of different strengths; some people are *very* strongly attracted to one another, while others are only mildly so. Accordingly, when one partner in a relationship happens to be attracted much more strongly to someone outside of the relationship than he or she is to the person inside of the relationship, there is a very strong chance that the existing relationship will eventually break up, because people tend to spontaneously "bond" with those individuals with whom they are the most strongly attracted.

Of course this isn't always the case. It is possible for a person to be very strongly attracted to someone outside of the marital relationship, and yet *not* leave the marital partner because of it. This can be due to a feeling of moral responsibility for one's marital partner, love for one's family, and the like. In such cases, though, the bonding strength with the extramarital individual is by definition not as strong as the bonding strength inside the marriage. Hence, when someone *does* come along who is able to attract a married person[33] in a much stronger fashion than the marital partner does, an eventual breakup becomes more likely (though it doesn't necessarily have to occur).

The point is simply that most people tend to end up in relationships where the strength of interpersonal bonding is the greatest. This is teleologically advantageous, because it makes it more likely that children—who need the presence of the two original parents whenever possible—will be born to strongly united couples, who will then be the least likely to break up in the future.

*Discussion*

People are often surprised to learn that most neurotics tend to be attracted to individuals who resemble one or both parents in some important way. To the extent that this observation is true, it shows just how important the neurotic's childhood struggles with his parents really were, *and are*, to him. They are so important, in fact, that he is romantically obsessed with them. He wants to fall in love with someone in the present so he can re-create, and hopefully resolve, his childhood parental conflicts which continue to haunt him.

Some people find it immensely distasteful to think that they are attracted to people that resemble, in some important way, the parent with whom they had the most conflict. Sam, for example, felt particularly fervent about this issue, "The only parental conflict I ever experienced in childhood was with my mother, but I can tell you that I would *never* be attracted to anyone who even *remotely* resembled her. I can't stand my mother. She makes me sick; so why would I ever be attracted to someone who was like her at all?"

The very intensity of Sam's response seemed to indicate that I had struck a sensitive nerve in Sam's private psychological life. If it were simply untrue, he would never have responded as profusely as he did. So I pressed the issue by asking him to describe those parts of his mother's personality that bothered him the most. He told me that it is was his mother's angry, overly-critical attitude that bothered him more than anything else. Nothing was apparently ever good enough for her, and this understandably made his skin crawl.

I then asked Sam to describe all the women that he had been in love with over the years. Remarkably enough, all of them shared one important quality: they were all angry, overly-critical people for whom nothing was ever good enough. Needless to say, Sam was floored by this important insight. He simply couldn't believe that he was attracted to women who were like his mother in this one relevant way.

It is sad realization indeed to learn that many people fall in love for motives that are largely selfish in nature. These individuals don't fall in love with someone because they truly admire who the person really is in the present. They simply fall in love with someone who happens to be able to fit into their own unconscious neurotic quagmire. In this sense, falling in love in this neurotic fashion is ultimately selfish by its very nature.

Of course, this isn't to say that we can't eventually come to love someone for who they really are, after we originally married them for selfish, neurotic reasons. We obviously can. More often than not, however, our neurotic enmeshment causes us just as many painful conflicts in the present as our parental struggles did in the past. As a result, those of us who are involved in neurotic relationships tend to fight with our romantic partners too much to be able to sustain a genuine love for them.

This leads us to still another reason why both men and women tend to feel so much hostility toward one another. To the extent that we have actually fallen in love with someone for the neurotic reasons mentioned above, we can never be truly happy, because we can never achieve the goal we are unconsciously striving for. Since the original pain that is tucked away in our unconscious is tied directly to our parents, and no one else, all the symbolic struggling in the world won't serve to resolve it. To attempt to do so would be like trying to put a fire out in Philadelphia by spraying water over the city of San Diego. No matter how much we struggle with our lover in the present, we will *always* be frustrated, because in the very process of this neurotic re-enactment, we can't help but transfer our original frustration with our parents onto our present-day lover. As a consequence, much of the hostility we experience in our present-day love life is simply a holdover from the hostility we experienced in childhood towards our parents, which in turn is compounded by the frustration we feel at trying to resolve the problem in the wrong way.

If we could only distinguish between past feelings towards our parents, on the one hand, and present-day feelings towards our lovers, on the other, we could then avoid most of the problems that we tend to experience in our romantic relationships. Unfortunately, this is a skill that relatively few individuals possess, because very few of us are actually aware of the difference between feelings rooted in the past and feelings rooted in the present. Most people simply assume that their present-day partner is the cause of all their current anger and hostility, when in fact much of it is probably originating in their unresolved conflicts from childhood.

The only way this particularly stubborn form of hostility can be overcome is through self-discipline and a commitment to resolve each of one's emotional conflicts on its own appropriate level. To do otherwise is to remain trapped within the self-deception of neurotic enslavement forever.

### A Case Study

When I first met Taylor, he was an alcoholic whose romantic life was a complete mess. Although he was off the bottle at last count and in therapy, he was still in an extremely vulnerable state, and has since come to realize that emotional recovery is in some sense an unending journey.

Taylor was born a healthy baby into a well-to-do family. Although his parents loved him immensely, they were incapable of translating this inner love into external behavior patterns that were conducive to Taylor's overall growth. His father, for instance, was an emotionally distant cardiologist who spent most of his waking hours in the hospital. Moreover, whenever his father was at home, he would almost completely tune Taylor out of his visual field, as if Taylor weren't even there. Although his father didn't deliberately *intend* to be so emotionally cold to his beloved son, he couldn't really help it, because he was a cold person by nature. Even so, Taylor heroically tried to get his father to listen to him almost every single night, but all to no avail. This understandably caused Taylor to feel as though he had nothing worthwhile to say; it also caused him to feel rejected, unloved, and worst of all, unlovable.

Taylor's mother wasn't much better. Although she was a much warmer person by nature than Taylor's father, she usually paid *too* much attention to Taylor. A classic overprotectionist, she wouldn't let Taylor do anything by himself. This gave Taylor a severe inferiority complex. Worst of all, the attention she gave him was primarily negative in nature, i.e., rather than telling him what he was doing right, she would instead concentrate on telling him what he was doing wrong. This only exacerbated Taylor's overall sense of inadequacy. It also convinced him that he would have to *earn* his love from both his parents, since they were clearly not loving him unconditionally for who *he* really was (at least not from a behavioral point of view).

Needless to say, these repeated bouts of negativity and rejection caused Taylor to experience severe episodes of emotional pain, which he instinctively proceeded to repress into his unconscious. Although this process of repression enabled Taylor to function relatively normally thoughout his childhood, it also caused him to become neurotic, so much so that by the time he entered high school, he was already experiencing physical symptoms from his neurosis. At first these symptoms were limited to severe migraine headaches and repeated episodes of colitis. Within a few months, though, Taylor fell into a full-blown psychic depression, which he proceeded to treat himself by taking whatever psychoactive drugs he could get his hands on.

It was as if Taylor instinctively realized that there was something ominous below the level of his conscious awareness that demanded his constant, undivided attention. Being a truth-seeker by nature, Taylor unknowingly found himself struggling to release these inner demons into his conscious awareness so he could find out their true identity. Eventually he succeeded. A bad reaction to marijuana one night overwhelmed the patency of his repressive lid, and he quickly developed a full-blown psychotic reaction, in which the contents of his unconscious mind came pouring out into his conscious awareness all at once. Although this breaking of his psychic floodgates caused Taylor to experience a tremendous amount of emotional agony, he was eventually able to *re-cover* most of his emotional pain and go on with a relatively normal drug-free life.

Unfortunately, Taylor continued to experience a residual amount of depression and anxiety from his bad drug experience. Although he successfully held a job as a computer programmer during this time period, his inner pain proceeded to get worse and worse, until eventually, Taylor turned to alcohol to help him get through the day. At first these drinking episodes were relatively minor and self-limited, but Taylor soon found that he couldn't function at all without alcohol.

His emotional instability during this time period was greatly exacerbated by his neurotic involvement with a woman who was just as cold to him as his father had been. This important similarity between his girlfriend and his father was just the "hook" he needed to fall "in love" with her almost instantaneously. Taylor described his initial meeting with Ellen in the following way:

> It was amazing. Although I was very depressed that night, my friends talked me into going to a certain party, so I went. The joviality at the party only made me *more* depressed, so I thought about leaving. But then it happened. I saw this beautiful woman across the room and knew *instantly* that she was the one for me. I mean, I *instantly* fell in love with her. I don't know how it happened, but it was definitely love at first sight, and it was *mutual*. We went out that night, and within a few hours, we became lovers.

Taylor was able to fall "in love" with Ellen so quickly because the interpersonal chemistry between them was ideal. Ellen was able to penetrate to the very core of Taylor's heart because she was very similar to the one person in Taylor's life who had meant the most to him: his own father. Because she had so many personality characteristics in common with Taylor's father, Taylor was able to respond to her in a very deep, family-like manner, because he was able to use her to carry on his childhood struggle for his father's love.

> I don't know what it is about Ellen, but I feel very different around her than I do around anyone else. We just feel "right" together; so much so, in fact, that I can really be myself around her, no matter what.

**65**

Taylor was able to be himself around Ellen because he was able to engage in the one activity with her that was more dear to him than anything else: the struggle for his father's love. Unfortunately, though, this profound level of intimacy also set the stage for an *extremely* dysfunctional relationship between them, because Taylor was unable to respond to Ellen entirely in the present. Since he was using a psychic memory pattern that was rooted deep in his past to deal with her, he was unable to respond to her as a unique and individual person in the present. As a result, they rapidly found themselves fighting almost daily.

> I don't know why Ellen started ticking me off so badly, but she just did. And it really wasn't anything she did to me by itself, because she never did anything horrendous to me, at least nothing that would justify my severe emotional reactions to her. I would just see red whenever she would do certain things, like ignore me while she was doing something else.

The reason Taylor got so incensed with Ellen was because she unconsciously reminded him of all the hurtful things that his father had done to him long ago. And since there was such an open line of communication between them, he felt free to express his inner pain to her (disguised as anger) in a way he never could to his father. This in turn made Ellen extremely angry, because she knew that she *couldn't* be responsible for causing the vast majority of Taylor's hostility reactions.

In addition, Taylor eventually came to feel tremendously frustrated with his lack of success at his unconscious struggle. The more he struggled, the less he seemed to get what he was struggling for. The reason for this, of course, is that *no* amount of struggling in the present with a romantic partner can eliminate the pain of being unloved as a child.

After several years of struggling in this manner, Taylor intuitively came to realize that his relationship with Ellen wasn't right for either of them. Even so, he felt an overwhelming emotional paralysis whenever it came time to break up with her.

> I knew I had to break up with her, but I just couldn't bring myself to do it. Every time I would try to tell her that we were through, a huge emotional void would overwhelm me, and I would simply give in and try to continue as normal.

The "emotional void" that Taylor felt whenever he tried to break up with Ellen was caused by his underlying fear of giving up hope for his father's precious love. Since Ellen was a father substitute for Taylor, the prospect of giving her up felt the same to him as giving up the struggle for his father's love, and this was something he was understandably loathe to do. No one wants to give up hope for the parental love that they never received as children, but this is nevertheless what must be done if emotional normality in this life is to ever be attained.

Even though Taylor refused to break up with Ellen, his inner conflict with her increasingly caused him to treat her worse and worse, so she eventually decided to leave *him*. This, of course, left Taylor with a tremendous amount of emotional pain deep inside, which he proceeded to drown out as much as possible with alcohol. After several years of being an almost perpetual drunk, Taylor found the courage to get off the bottle and to enter therapy. He is now attempting to work through his old parental feelings with the aid of his therapist. If he can succeed in doing this, his future looks promising.

# The Role of Projection and Scapegoating

IT IS A WELL-KNOWN FACT IN THE PSYCHOANALYTIC LITERATURE that human beings have a strong tendency to project their own faults and inadequacies onto other people. Although such an act is neurotic by definition, it serves one important function in the individual's psychological economy: it helps to preserve the ego from potentially damaging self-attack.

When a person is in a situation where he is guilty of some form of wrongdoing, he can do one of three possible things:
1) he can take full responsibility for his own error,
2) he can project his guilt onto someone else and then blame them for it, or
3) he can totally deny that any wrongdoing has ever taken place.

Very few individuals are consistently strong enough to be able to take full responsibility for their own wrong actions. It is much easier to simply deny the problem, or to unconsciously project it onto someone else and then blame them for it.

Whenever the latter "solution" is engaged in, it is called *scapegoating*. A scapegoat is simply an innocent individual who has been arbitrarily chosen by someone else to be the recipient of that person's own guilt and critical blame. Hitler, for instance, repeatedly used the Jews as his unwilling scapegoats.

Scapegoating utilizes the psychological process of *psychic projection* to make people feel better. There are three reasons why scapegoating tends to have this effect:
1) it provides the welcome illusion that one's former problem has already disappeared,
2) it places the blame elsewhere in order to help diminish one's own sense of guilt, and
3) it gives the person the satisfaction of feeling like he has punished the wrongdoing.

Men who identify with the Macho Ideal are particularly susceptible to this kind of scapegoating behavior. Since the Macho Ideal contains the explicit belief that the human male is blameless and nearly perfect, a man who sincerely believes in its validity can't bear to accept full responsibility for most of his wrong actions, because this would directly contradict the dictates of the Macho Ideal. Therefore, since he must strive to be perfect and blameless in order to be a "real man," he finds that he must project his guilt onto someone else so he can blame them, and thereby help to dissipate his *own* guilt feelings. This is why macho men tend to be so unreasonable and hotheaded, no matter how good people are to them: because they are routinely blaming everyone around them for their *own* wrongdoing.

### Negative Anima Projection

As we noted earlier, the anima represents the feminine region in a man's psyche. Among other things, it is responsible for causing foul moods in men. This usually occurs when a man's "inner woman" becomes dissatisfied with the way he is leading his life. As a consequence, the anima typically brings a dark, foreboding mood over him, seemingly out of nowhere, which he is usually at a total loss to explain. Predictably, though, he will try to find someone convenient to blame for his bad mood, because it usually doesn't occur to him that he alone could be responsible for causing it.

When such an anima-possessed individual is in relationship with a woman, she will often be the unconscious recipient of this type of negative anima projection from him, because, as we have seen, the anima tends to be projected onto an appropriate person whenever it possibly can, especially in negative circumstances. When this is actually the case, the woman herself will typically be perceived as the cause of the man's bad mood. This of course leads almost invariably to a major confrontation between the two parties, because no one likes to be made to suffer at the hands of another. It doesn't matter that the woman in these instances is totally innocent as far as the man's bad mood is concerned, because the anima-possessed man really and truly *thinks* that she is responsible for causing it.

This represents yet another major cause of male hostility reactions toward women. When a man can't live in peace with his own anima, he unconsciously tends to project his resulting animosity out onto the significant women in his life, which in turn leads to spontaneous (and unwarranted) hostility reactions against them.

In a worst case scenario, the negative anima projection can be so severe that the female recipient can actually be perceived in terms of the familiar witch image. This explains how so many innocent women in the past could have been burned at the stake as witches: they were the unwilling recipients of profoundly negative anima projections from men.

Today, however, women hardly fare any better. Though they are no longer being burned at the stake as witches, they are still being treated just as monstrously in other ways, because they are still the unfortunate recipients of negative anima projections from men. Women are beaten, tortured, raped, and killed by men on a daily basis, and all because of the same male psychological defect that caused the infamous witch-hunts of the late 1600's.

It is a sad commentary on the human condition that so many innocent women have been forced to suffer at the hands of unrestrained male psychopathology over the years. However, now that the underlying cause of the problem is largely understood, we can hopefully begin to make some headway into getting the problem resolved once and for all. Unfortunately, "men still will be men," no matter how much we understand male psychopathology. There simply seems to be no way to escape the intrinsic demands of the human developmental process, even if it means that millions of innocent people will be forced to suffer as a result.

## Treatment

The best way to deal with this type of male hostility is through education and deliberate consciousness-raising. Scapegoating men desperately need to become aware of the fact that they are harming other people's lives for their own pathological gain. The hope here is that if these macho individuals can come to an understanding of *how* they are mistaken, they might be able to break out of their incredibly destructive neurotic habit.

Since it is usually quite difficult for a woman to educate her husband or boyfriend about this kind of thing, it is often best for the scapegoating man to seek professional counseling for his mental aberrance. The difficult part, of course, is convincing him that he needs to see a therapist in the first place.

## The Phenomenon of Romantic Projection

In my previous book *Why Men Cheat*, I showed how the phenomenon of romantic projection is probably the greatest reason why men are driven to cheat on their wives. As it turns out, the process of romantic projection is *also* one of the most important reasons why men tend to feel so much hostility toward women.

In the process of romantic projection, people unknowingly project their own desires for personal fulfillment onto their romantic partner. The purpose of this complex psychological maneuver is to seek psychospiritual wholeness vicariously though the other person, and *not*

**71**

through oneself. However, when this occurs, the projecting individual can't help but be eventually disappointed, because no mere mortal can bring complete psychospiritual fulfillment to another. The projecting individual, however, *expects* his partner to give him this precious fulfillment. Therefore, when she fails to do so, he tends to get angry at her for withholding his happiness from him. This leads to yet another vicious cycle of hostility and open fighting.

We in the West need to learn to take full responsibility for our own psychic fulfillment and personal happiness. We need to learn that no one else besides ourselves can give us the parts of our personalities that we are missing deep inside. When this momentous concept is fully realized and subsequently acted upon, a new stage of interpersonal intimacy can then be initiated, in which we no longer blame our partners for our own lack of inner development. Instead, we will voluntarily do whatever is necessary to contribute to our own growth and well-being. This owning up to the responsibilities of our own development will undoubtedly reduce the amount of hostility that we feel towards our romantic partners, because we will then no longer be placing any unrealistic demands upon them. This in turn will produce relationships that are far more harmonious and fulfilling than anything else we will have ever previously experienced.

# Love and the Grand Male Deception

THUS FAR WE HAVE EXPLORED A NUMBER OF REASONS WHY the macho male tends to feel hostility towards the opposite sex. We have also seen how some men are so consumed with this hostility that they actually hate women deep inside. Ironically, though, a significant proportion of these misogynists outwardly act as though they *love* women; some are even so charming that they are colloquially known as womanizers.

Predictably, the origins of this grand male deception extend to the innermost regions of the human psyche. We will now devote our attention towards understanding where this fraudulent behavior comes from and how it can be overcome once and for all.

### The Reaction Formation

It is a well-known fact that humans often behave in a manner that is directly opposite to their true inner reality. In the Freudian psychoanalytic literature this is called a *reaction formation*, and it constitutes one of the ways in which the mind defends itself against pain and anxiety. In order to escape the burden of feeling a certain way, we often act in a manner that is directly *opposite* to how we really feel deep inside.

For example, an individual who feels weak and incompetent on the inside may unconsciously attempt to defend himself from this unpleasant state of affairs by acting strong and and competent on the outside. The intensity of this external show of strength is often directly proportional to the degree of insecurity that is felt on the inside: the more insecure an individual tends to feel on the inside, the more intense his show of strength tends to be on the outside. This may be one reason why it is said that "the bigger they are, the harder they fall." If people tend to act big because they feel little on the inside, then the bigger people act, the smaller they probably feel on the inside, which in turn means the harder they will probably fall when they are actually attacked.

### Two Reasons for Male Deception

Given this preliminary overview, there are two primary reasons that can be given for why women-hating men tend to pretend as though they love women. First and foremost, this outer show of love typically entails a reaction formation designed to help the individual alleviate intense feelings of guilt.

Whether they know it or not, many human beings tend to feel uncomfortable when they consciously experience hatred or hostility towards other people. The extent of this discomfort is often related to the overall appropriateness of one's hostility response, vis-à-vis the actual behavior of the individual to whom one's hostility is directed. For instance, if someone is actually deserving of a major hostility response (such as the pedophiliac who molests one's children), then one will probably not feel very guilty about feeling anger and hostility towards this person. On the other hand, if one is simply taking out one's inner anger on another innocent person, then one is much more likely to feel guilty about it (because this kind of behavior is clearly pathological and inappropriate).

This same sort of rationale can also be applied to the misogynist. For as we have seen, almost every one of the reasons why men tend to hate women is rooted in the various shortcomings of the *male* psyche, and *not* in any specific behavior patterns of females per se. While most misogynists may not be consciously aware of their own responsibility for their behavior, they seem to be *unconsciously* aware of it. This is apparently where most of the misogynist's underlying guilt actually comes from.

This being the case, the typical woman-hater will naturally want to do everything in his power to get rid of his inner guilt. One of the most effective ways of doing this, as we have seen, is by engaging in an unconscious *reaction formation*, where the misogynist outwardly acts as though he loves women in order to attenuate his feelings of guilt about hating them so badly.

Let us take Bill's behavior toward Emily as an illustration. For a variety of reasons, Bill felt an inordinate amount of hostility toward *all* women, which, of course, included his girlfriend Emily. Moreover, Bill routinely experienced a number of *specific* hostility reactions towards Emily, each of which was rooted in the neurotic trappings of his own psyche. Yet, Bill felt very uncomfortable about all of his anger, especially because Emily rarely did anything to deserve it. As a consequence, Bill felt compelled to make up for his underlying hatred of women by being as nice to Emily as he possibly could. He routinely cooked for her, cleaned her house, washed her clothes, and wined and dined her in a way that would make any woman envious.

Nevertheless, his motives were not genuine, since he was only being nice to her in order to alleviate his *own* feelings of guilt and hostility, not because he truly felt like being nice for its own sake. As always, his latent hostility still expressed itself in a variety of other, more indirect ways. For one thing, his hostility caused him to continually put off making a marital commitment with Emily, which is the one thing she really wanted from him. As Bill himself put it, "I couldn't imagine getting married to Emily, not because I don't love her, but because I think I harbor far too many negative feelings towards her—and towards *all* women—to actually tie the knot."

Even more ominous was Bill's compulsion to secretly sleep with other women in order to help him vent his hate and hostility toward Emily. This all-too-frequent method of handling inner anger forced Bill to lead a dual lifestyle, in which he had to chronically lie to Emily in order to keep from being found out. No wonder he has continually complained about being so chronically frustrated and unhappy in his day-to-day life!

Fortunately, the solution for this predicament is as easily described as the problem: if a man's hostility toward women is the primary cause of his interpersonal unhappiness, then the only method of treatment that can eliminate this problem once and for all is the complete eradication of his underlying hostility. As usual, this is much easier said than done, but it can still be accomplished with enough desire and perseverance.

The second reason why misogynists pretend they love women is for the sheer practicality of the moment. If a man openly acts out his inner hostility toward women, the only type of woman that will put up with him is an out-and-out masochist. Everyone else will avoid him like the plague, and he, in turn, will lose out on his goal of "landing a catch."

As a consequence, the inwardly hostile male who is strongly motivated to go to bed with a woman will do everything in his power to persuade her to sleep with him, no matter how hostile he may feel on the inside. He will be "nice" to her, buy her expensive gifts, and take her out to the finest restaurants, all so he can maximize his chances of getting her to go to bed with him. In reality, though, he will still be hostile on the inside, and this hostility will in all likelihood end up revealing itself after he finally gets what he wants.

# The Male Hostility Quotient

It isn't very difficult to determine whether or not a given male is experiencing a significant degree of hostility toward women. One need only consider his past behavior in a variety of circumstances in order to make this determination.

With this in mind, I've come up with the following test to determine a man's overall "Hostility Quotient." Its purpose is to help the reader ascertain the degree to which a man is experiencing hostility toward women.

*Determining Your Overall Hostility Quotient*

Read each of the following questions carefully and try to answer them as honestly as possible. Give yourself (or the man under scrutiny, if you are a woman) a:

>> 4 if your answer is "very often"; a
>> 3 if your answer is "somewhat often"; a
>> 2 if your answer is "sometimes"; a
>> 1 if your answer is "rarely," and a
>> 0 if your answer is "never."

Be sure to double your point totals on those questions where this is indicated (i.e., if your answer to a question in which doubling is indicated is "very often," give yourself an 8 instead of a 4).

1. I tend to view the women in my life as obstacles to be overcome in my quest for happiness. 2
2. I think a woman should do anything within her power to make her man happy, even if it means sacrificing a significant amount of her own happiness. 1
3. I feel like I want to lash out and slap my wife/girlfriend whenever we argue.
4. I actually *do* slap her or push her around when I get upset with her (Double Point Question).
5. I sometimes fantasize about physically beating my wife/girlfriend in order to put her in her place.
6. I actually *do* beat her up quite severely from time to time (Double Point Question).
7. I think men should have precedence over women in virtually all circumstances in life.

8. I think the women's liberation movement over the last couple of decades has been a useless and worthless venture.
9. I think I should have the freedom to go out on my wife/girlfriend from time to time if it makes me happy.
10. I do *not* think my wife/girlfriend has the similar right to go out on me.
11. I strongly identify with sexist humor, such as that propagated by Andrew Dice Clay or Sam Kinison.
12. I often call women "bitches," "sluts," "whores," or worse.

Add up your total number of points, and then compare the sum with the following chart:

| Numerical Total | Hostility Quotient |
| --- | --- |
| A) 48-56 | You have a very severe problem that needs immediate professional attention. |
| B) 39-47 | You have a severe problem that should be dealt with as soon as possible. |
| C) 30-38 | The "high normal" (i.e., extremely typical) range for most American males. Nevertheless, it is still very pathological, so professional treatment is still very strongly indicated. |
| D) 21-29 | The "low to mid-normal" range for most American males. Since it is still pathological, professional treatment is strongly recommended. |
| E) 12-20 | The "very low to low normal" range for most American males. Although this degree of hostility is comparatively slight, it nevertheless indicates that some degree of pathology is still present. Consequently, you could still benefit from intensive self-work or even professional treatment. |
| F) 7-11 | You have a much lower degree of hostility toward women than the average American male, but you still may harbor a significant amount of anger deep inside. |
| G) 0-6 | The ideal male. This is the goal of relative non-hostility toward women that all men should be striving for. |

# Overcoming the Hostility Trap

*The Damaging Effects of Hostility*

Negative emotions, such as hatred, hostility, guilt, and the like, are known to cause a wide variety of physical and emotional problems. Numerous epidemiological studies have linked these negative emotions to heart disease, mental illness, and even cancer.

A decade ago, it was simply thought that the "Type A" personality—the individual who is chronically anxious, driven, and ambitious—is the one who is at significantly greater risk for degenerative disease. Today, however, it is known that it isn't being anxious or driven per se that causes greater risk; it is the *hostility* that is often present in classic Type A personalities that is *itself* to blame.

This is the conclusion of University of Maryland psychologist Theodore M. Dembroski, who has studied Type A personalities for over 15 years. According to Dembroski, chronically hostile individuals are up to two-and-a-half times more likely to die from heart disease than those who are more relaxed.

The reason for this sorry state of affairs has to do with the physiological stress that is generated in the body in response to chronic hostility. Angry emotions cause adrenaline and cortisone—the body's stress hormones—to be released in excessive quantities into the bloodstream, where they then proceed to wreak all sorts of biochemical havoc on the body's various organ systems. At the micro level, these stress hormones tend to "auto-oxidize" into harmful "free radicals," which are then able to selectively attack the body's cell membranes, DNA, and even its entire immune system.

Free radicals are those mischevious biochemical entities which gerontologists and other researchers are now implicating in the genesis of those degenerative diseases associated with the aging process. Although the body constantly manufactures its own free radicals in response to normal physiological processes, it is only equipped to safely handle a certain number of them. Thus, when chronic stress causes the body to produce an unusually large number of free radicals, the body's "anti-oxidant defense system" quickly becomes overwhelmed, and excessive numbers of free radicals are allowed to attack the various cells of the body. Over time, this stress-induced process results in degenerative diseases such as atherosclerosis and cancer.[34]

Chronically hostile individuals also tend to have higher blood pressures and faster pulse rates than the normal population. This of course puts *additional* stress on the heart. Over time, this chronic "fight or flight" response causes the heart's muscle fibers to wear out. It also causes serious damage to the coronary arteries that supply the heart with blood.

The cumulative effect of this physiological and biochemical stress is that the chronically hostile individual is like a walking time-bomb, insofar as he is at a *much* greater risk of dying from some sort of degenerative disease. And when we also consider the fact that these individuals are more likely to drink, smoke, be sedentary, and be addicted to a high-fat, high-cholesterol diet, it's a wonder that they live as long as they do.

It isn't hard correlating the damaging effects of chronic hostility to health problems in men. We've known for a long time that males have a significantly shorter lifespan than females in the West. We've also known that men tend to experience more hostility overall than women, and that they tend to handle their hostility in more self-destructive ways. Indeed, this may be the most important risk factor of all in the relationship between hostility and degenerative disease. Keeping one's anger and hostility bottled in, as men are more likely to do, is known to be *extremely* damaging to the entire body. "Letting it all hang out," on the other hand, is known to be far less destructive. And now that scientists are finally finding a strong causal link between hostility and degenerative disease, there can no longer be any doubt: *chronic hostility is lethal, and so should be avoided at all cost.*

At one time, psychosomatic medicine—which is the study of how the mind affects the body, and vice versa—was regarded with suspicion by the orthodox medical establishment. Drawing on the absolute Cartesian dualism between mind and body, traditional medical practitioners found it hard to see how the mind could affect the health of the body, or how the body could affect the health of the mind. Today, however, things are radically different. The fledgling science of psychoneuroimmunology—which deals with the effect of the emotions on physical and mental health—is now one of the hottest topics in modern medical research. Numerous studies have shown beyond reasonable doubt that one's emotional state can have a *profound* effect on the status of one's physical and mental health.

Actually, we should have known all along that the mind is capable of exerting a profound influence on the body. Doctors have used placebos, which are nothing more than inert sugar pills, for years to effect positive clinical results. Numerous physical ailments ranging from arthritis to lupus are known to respond well to placebo treatment. Even withdrawing heroin addicts have been known to become sedated when given a placebo which they think is a narcotic.

Of course, this shouldn't be taken to mean that these physical ailments are all imaginary. It simply means that one's mental and emotional attitude can exert *extremely* far-reaching effects on one's state of physical health.

African practitioners of voodoo have long been aware of this intriguing relationship between mind and body. Using the power of belief alone, they have the documented ability to cause others to become sick, or to even die, simply through the implantation of negative beliefs and emotions into their minds. The voodoo curse of death, for instance, apparently involves little more than convincing someone that, at such and such a time, he or she will physically die. And as long as the cursed individual really and truly believes this, the odds are very good indeed that death will actually occur on schedule.

In a similar, though opposite vein, it has been known for years that people who are gravely ill often have the remarkable ability to delay their expiration until an important event, such as an anniversary or birthday, has taken place. If the mind had little or no control over the body, we would never expect this to happen. Yet, it *does* in fact happen, and quite frequently at that.

The incredible power of belief in determining the body's overall health status is a recurring theme in many different religions. Jesus, for instance, repeatedly taught that "as a man believes in his heart, so is he." He also confined his miracles of healing to those who really and truly *believed* they could be healed.

Some people like to point to their own sick bodies as evidence that mere belief alone is incapable of working miracles. While this may be true, it might also be true that negative attitudes and emotions may be preventing any significant healing from taking place. This is known as *self-fulfilling prophecy*: by believing that such and such is the case, we often tend to make our inner belief come true, not necessarily because it is *independently* true, but because it can *become* true if we believe in it strong enough. This is because a sufficiently powerful belief automatically tends to motivate us to behave in such a way as to make certain consequences, predicted by the belief, come true. This fact in and of itself should be sufficient to convince us of the enormous power of belief in human life.

The point of this discussion is simply to show that people who harbor significant quantities of hostility, hate, and resentment deep inside of them need to be healed of these negative emotions *before* they can ever hope to be happy and healthy in their day-to-day lives. Thus, there are two powerful incentives for hostile people to get rid of their hostility: the promise of greatly improved romantic relations, and the promise of greatly improved physical and mental health.

### A Step-By-Step Guide for Eradicating Hostility From One's Life

The first step in eliminating hostility toward women (or toward anyone) is becoming aware of the problem. It is next to impossible for anyone to resolve a problem that they never knew they had, because the various techniques that one must use to eradicate hostility are themselves based on an intimate awareness of the underlying problem.

It is at this point that the hostile male often reaches his first major bottleneck in the quest for a hostility-free life. The radical nature of the Macho Ideal tends to make it very difficult for those men who espouse it to even go so far as to *admit* to themselves or to others that they have a problem. As you will recall, one of the chief presuppositions of the Macho Ideal is the goal of complete self-sufficiency. Part and parcel with this goal is the desire to be completely free from error. Thus, the truly macho individual is both totally self-sufficient and completely free from error in his day-to-day life.

This is why it is so difficult to get the genuinely macho individual to admit that he has a problem: because the internal dictates of the Macho Ideal are incompatible with even the barest admission of weakness or personal insufficiency. This is where the constructive value of suffering comes in handy. For as long as the macho individual is living a pleasurable, hassle-free life, he won't feel compelled to admit that he has a problem. The tremendous hubris that is fostered by the Macho Ideal makes it next to impossible for this critical admission to occur; that is, as long as the hubris is still intact.

Interestingly enough, nothing eradicates personal hubris quite as effectively as physical and emotional suffering. This is a doctrine that the major religious traditions of the world have been teaching for centuries. Pain is the ultimate antidote for pride, which itself is the poison that prevents millions of people from being happy and from reaching their true potential in life.

**82**

Fortunately, attempting to live in accordance with the Macho Ideal often causes enough suffering in and of itself to make even the most stoic of men think twice about their own self-sufficiency. It isn't easy harboring hostility and sexist prejudice in one's innermost self each and every day of one's life. It's like carrying around an emotional volcano everywhere one goes. Even if one is able to contain one's emotional eruptions to the point that they are not visible to most people, they still can cause more than enough suffering in one's life to make one miserable.

The first step, then, on the road to recovery is the admission that one has a problem. Just like the alcoholic who cannot begin to kick the habit until he first admits he has a problem, the hostile male cannot begin to travel down the road to recovery until he admits that he has a problem.

Once this admission takes place, the second step involves the complete re-education of his macho attitude toward life. For as long as he continues to believe in the validity of the Macho Ideal, even on a deep, unconscious level, true recovery will be impossible.

As we have seen, the cognitive roots of the Macho Ideal are so pervasive that they extend to virtually every aspect of a man's self-image and attitude towards the world. Thus, to re-educate a man to think and feel in a non-macho way typically entails far more than simple education; it necessitates a complete brainwashing or erasure of his former belief structure, so that a completely new one can take its place. As the Bible teaches, one cannot put new wine into old wineskins, because the old wineskins will either break or end up polluting the new wine. Rather, one must put new wine into *new* wineskins, so that it can be properly contained.

What this means in terms of the re-education of the macho man is that he must experience a type of psychological rebirth before he can create a proper "container" for his new beliefs and attitudes. Since his old character structure was originally formed in accordance with the dictates of the Macho Ideal, it *cannot* serve as a suitable container for these new non-macho beliefs. Most males, then, must experience a complete psychological rebirth before they will be able to successfully shed the restrictive yoke of their former machismo.

Fortunately, the very pain that tends to break down the macho man's pride in his own self-sufficiency often tends to completely reform his entire character structure at the same time. Moreover, the non-macho beliefs and attitudes that are an integral part of the macho man's re-education are *themselves* so powerful that they can also help to transform the macho man's old character structure into a new and exciting kind of personality.

This non-macho cognitive set has received a great deal of press in the years since "male liberation" first became fashionable. This "new man of the 90's" is a sensitive and introspective sort who isn't afraid to feel or to admit his own shortcomings. Moreover, he isn't nearly as sick as his earlier macho counterpart, because he isn't harboring any unreasonable hostilities towards the opposite sex. He also isn't hopelessly trying to stick to some impossible ideal, in the hope that he will eventually be able to attain it. This alone makes him a good deal happier and more relaxed than he ever could have been otherwise. In short, this new, non-macho individual is one of the first men in recent history to experience what true manhood was originally meant to be like, unfettered by unreasonable expectations and impossible ideals.

### Anti-Hostility Therapy

Psychiatrist Milton Layden's Anti-Hostility Therapy can also be employed to help defuse the macho man's hostility towards the opposite sex. According to Layden, the best way to overcome the hostility trap in almost every area of life is to think realistically about each and every stage of the hostility-building reaction.[35]

First and foremost, Layden encourages us to realize that deep inside, we're neither inferior to other people, nor superior to them. As human beings, we're all more or less *equal* in this regard. While many people have talents that cannot be duplicated by others, *everyone* has some sort of talent, whether it is obvious or not. On the whole, though, we're all still equal in terms of our intrinsic rights as human beings. Nevertheless, we're all inevitably disrespected by others from time to time, and this tends to make us feel inferior in our innermost selves.

These feelings of inferiority have two basic causes: either

1) we did something *ourselves* to warrant the disrespectful treatment, in which case it is merely something we *did* that was inferior, *and not our own selves*, or

2) the person who disrespected us did so because he had something bad happen to *him*, in which case we are not responsible for his angry behavior at all.

In this latter case, Layden tells us that we should actually feel sorry for the person who disrespects us, not be angry with him.

In either of the above cases, though, there is no rational basis for the belief that we are intrinsically inferior as individuals. If we are genuinely at fault in our behavior, we should welcome the criticism as an opportunity for change, under the overall rubric that people who make innocent mistakes are not inherently inferior at all.[36] However, if we as persons are *not* at fault in our behavior, then we should feel *sympathy* for the person who is acting in a hostile fashion towards us, not inferior or angry.

Going one step further, just as there is no rational basis for feelings of inherent inferiority in life, there is also no rational basis for feelings of inherent superiority, especially the kind that is engendered by the Macho Ideal. We all need to strive to be humble individuals who are neither more, nor less, privileged than any of our fellow humans. It is clear that when this Ideal of Social Equality is consciously adhered to, the opportunities for hostility reactions towards others become vastly reduced, for when there are no superiority feelings, there is also no unrealistic bubble of pride that can burst when one is confronted with disrespectful behavior from others.

However, it is equally clear that one cannot jettison feelings of superiority and simultaneously adhere to the dictates of the Macho Ideal. The very *essence* of this macho goal is defined by a man's alleged superiority over the opposite sex. Therefore, one cannot cannot develop an equitable mind set towards others and still pay homage to the Macho Ideal. The two simply cannot coexist together. We see, then, that the very superiority that is engendered by the Macho Ideal is *itself* an instrumental factor in the etiology of the male hostility reaction, especially towards women.

Layden's ideas concerning the relationship of hostility reactions to inferiority feelings are particularly relevant to this discussion. According to Layden, humans tend to react with hostility whenever they feel inferior deep inside. However, as long as a man believes in the impossible dictates of the Macho Ideal, he is *bound* to feel inferior, because no one can *possibly* live their life in accordance with such a ridiculous standard of behavior. *This is perhaps the greatest reason of all why macho-oriented men tend to react with so much hostility towards the opposite sex: because their allegiance to the Macho Ideal inevitably makes them feel inferior deep inside, and inferiority feelings naturally give rise to overt hostility reactions in people.*

**85**

It follows, then, that if one simply discards the unrealistic standards imposed by the Macho Ideal and realizes that there is no rational basis whatsoever for feeling either superior or inferior in life, one will no longer be prone to unrealistic hostility reactions, especially towards women.

### The Role of Emotional Purging in the New Male Transformation

Earlier we saw that one of the most potent sources of hostility in the male psyche is generated from within the unconscious itself, in response to all the repressed pains and fears that have been stored in it since childhood. To the extent that we must continually exert energy to keep these past traumas repressed, we are going to experience two unpleasant side effects:

1) we are going to feel far more drained and depleted than we would otherwise feel, and

2) we are going to subjectively experience the pressure of these repressed pains as anger, hostility, or depression (depending on the strength of our repressive capacity and on our own idiosyncratic way of responding to this intra-psychic stress).

Indeed, many individuals are, for one reason or another, unable to keep their repressed feelings completely at bay. As a consequence, bits and pieces of their subjugated feelings are eventually able to make their way into consciousness, where they subsequently act to severely distort their mental state.

Most typically, this type of emotional intrusion from the past leads to depression, as one struggles to "de-press" the liberated pain back into the unconscious, where it seems to belong. Oftentimes, though, this depressive reaction can give way to a full-blown hostility response, as one spontaneously reacts with open anger to the emotional pain that one experienced during childhood.

The underlying code of ethics specified by the Macho Ideal only acts to exacerbate this potential hostility response. It tells a man that he is supposed to be emotionally impervious to all external threats that are directed at him, and that, moreover, he should be able to succeed in his life no matter how many times he is threatened from without.

In reality, though, the man who is being confronted by his repressed emotions finds himself suffering intensely on an almost daily basis, directly at the hands of his own past history. This suffering creates a vital tension between the way things really are in his life, and the way things *ought to be*, as specified by the Macho Ideal. The greater this discrepancy between the "is" and the "ought" in a man's life, the more disturbed he is liable to feel.

This disturbance is exacerbated by the underlying presuppositions of the Macho Ideal, which dictate the conditions that must be satisfied if an individual is to be considered a "real man." Since emotional vulnerability is most definitely *not* one of these defining conditions, it follows that any male who is under emotional duress is not a "real man." Thus, any emotionally vulnerable male who unconsciously accepts the validity of the Macho Ideal must choose between two very difficult options. On the one hand, he can conclude that the Macho Ideal is a false ethical standard, in which case he must then find another way to define his own manhood. On the other hand, he can continue to believe in the validity of the Macho Ideal, in which case he must then conclude that he never was a "real man" to begin with.

Unfortunately, most men are exceedingly reluctant to even *question* the underlying dictates of the Macho Ideal. They figure that since they were indoctrinated with these values from the very beginning, the values themselves *must* be right. This reluctance to give up the Macho Ideal encourages the emotionally distraught male to conclude that he isn't a "real man" after all, and this understandably tends to lead to a full-blown hostility response.

Sadly, most people who are suffering at the hands of their repressions tend to be unaware of the historical nature of their pain. They figure that since they are suffering in the midst of present-day circumstances, the ultimate cause of their pain must be located in the present as well. This simply isn't true at all, but this fact doesn't prevent most people from "projecting" their past pain onto the present.

This confusion of the past with the present is fostered by the reality that certain people in the present can act as emotional *triggers* for the spontaneous release of old repressed feelings in susceptible individuals. When these susceptible individuals see that certain people in the present are capable of eliciting powerful negative emotions within them, they are strongly tempted to believe that these individuals are actually *causing* their reactions. In reality, though, they are only triggering them to experience feelings that they already possess deep inside. This confusion of past feelings with present-day circumstances understandably leads to all sorts of problems in our interpersonal relationships, since no one likes to be blamed for things they're not responsible for.

The point is simply that as long as a person remains overly repressed, he or she will be unable to completely overcome the hostility trap, because there will always be some need to vent emotional "steam" from inside one's unconscious. This is why any hostility-reducing program *must* effectively deal with these repressed pains; otherwise, it is almost certain to fail.

As Janov has pointed out, all the talk therapy in the world can never eliminate the negative effects of these repressed pains, because the repressions themselves remain as intact as the first day they were laid down, and it is these repressions that are the cause of all the trouble. According to Janov, there is only one way to get rid of these unconscious "demons": by allowing ourselves to "go back" into the past, so to speak, so we can finish feeling those horrible pains that were spontaneously aborted when we were young children.

The reason why this is so gets back to what seems to be a fundamental law of human consciousness. *Every emotion that is elicited in the human psyche must be completely and totally experienced, no matter how painful it happens to be, in order for psychological health to be maintained.* If it isn't, then the aborted feeling itself will remain frozen within the unconscious in the same form in which it was abandoned years ago, where it will be anxiously awaiting the opportunity to re-enter consciousness so it can finish playing itself out. This is why these repressed feelings tend to wreak such havoc in our minds: because they are continually struggling to escape from their unconscious prison. In the process, they can't help but disturb our state of consciousness, which, as Ernest Becker has so aptly pointed out, is specifically *designed* to keep these unconscious elements at bay.

A good way to visualize the dynamics of emotional repression is in terms of an exploding firecracker. A painful childhood feeling can be likened to an exploding firecracker, insofar as both can cause intense pain if they are directly experienced. The act of repression itself, though, is like aborting the firecracker's explosion in the middle of its actual detonation, since it abruptly terminates a painful emotional experience and consigns it to the unconscious. But just as the aborted firecracker explosion naturally "wants" to finish the act of exploding, each aborted feeling that we banish to the unconscious also "wants" to complete its own original "explosion" as well. As long as we prevent this from happening, we are prone to experience all manner of psychopathology, not the least of which is chronic hostility and psychic depression. Consequently, the way to emotional recovery *requires* that we allow these repressions back into consciousness one at a time, so we can finish feeling them once and for all, for this is the only way they can be resolved forever.

Although many therapeutic techniques have arisen in recent years to allegedly help rid the unconscious of its many repressions, the best remains Janov's own Primal Institute in Los Angeles. The staff at the Primal Institute have been specially trained in a wide variety of effective therapeutic techniques, which enable them to safely and effectively drain the mind of its repressed contents.

Unfortunately, not everyone can afford the tremendous cost of entering Primal Therapy. Although several other mock primal therapies can be found in almost every major city of the United States, there is no way to guarantee their safety or efficacy.

There is, however, a form of Primal Therapy that one can perform on oneself, in which it is possible for one to purge oneself of one's own unconscious contents in the privacy of one's own home, either alone or with a trusted companion. Although one is much better off working directly with a therapist who has been trained in this type of "implosive" therapy (due to the inherent difficulty of the primal process itself), this isn't always possible or practical. However, with a little instruction and the proper attitude, it is possible to perform Primal Therapy on oneself. The reason for this, of course, is that the liberation of the unconscious is a natural event that tends to happen *spontaneously* whenever our conscious controls are abandoned.

For the sake of those individuals who want to attempt this type of emotional purging on their own, I will now present the following protocol for a self-administered cleansing of the unconscious. Before doing so, however, I should hasten to point out that attempting to perform Primal Therapy on one's own self can have dangerous and even tragic consequences if it is done improperly, since it is like performing emotional surgery on oneself. THEREFORE, ONE SHOULD ONLY DO SO AT ONE'S OWN DISCRETION AND SELF-ACKNOWLEDGED RISK.

*A Protocol for Performing Primal Therapy on Oneself*

The best time to attempt to purge oneself of one's past emotional pains is when one is feeling down and depressed. This is because the depressed feeling itself is part of the underlying repression that needs to be liberated. Thus, the more depressed one feels, the closer one actually is to the old feeling that needs to be purged. This is why Janov can say that depressed people are actually *closer* to true mental health than "normal" repressed people are: because they are closer to purging themselves of their own past pains. Indeed, the whole reason why depression feels so bad in the first place is because a relatively small portion of a repressed feeling has leaked over into consciousness. This produces a crippling type of emotional paralysis, because the divided feeling can neither be completely felt (in which case it would be resolved), nor completely repressed.

Primal Therapy seeks to eliminate this depressive agony by bringing the *entire* feeling into conscious awareness, where it can then be completely experienced and subsequently resolved. The basic idea of Primal Therapy, then, is for the "patient" to go back into his or her past, as it were, so he or she can finish feeling those painful emotional experiences that were spontaneously aborted during childhood.

Unfortunately, this process is much easier said than done. Humans have a natural aversion to experiencing the contents of their own unconscious, because of the inordinately painful feelings that tend to reside there. In fact, this is why these old feelings were originally repressed to begin with: precisely *because* they were so painful.

Indeed, as Ernest Becker has pointed out in *The Denial of Death*, we humans are so obsessed with keeping these old pains repressed that our entire personalities have inadvertently been organized around this "vital lie of character." As a consequence, it takes a *tremendous* amount of courage and determination (if not outright desperation) to be able to force oneself to face and relive these old horrors, especially if one feels like one doesn't have to. This is why it is so difficult to undergo a genuine primal experience without the aid of a specially trained Primal Therapist: because it is profoundly difficult for most people to overcome their own inner resistance without outside help.

Thus, the first step to be overcome in the liberation of one's unconscious is the natural resistance of the mind to facing the contents of its own "emotional dungeon." This is exceedingly difficult without the aid of a determined Primal Therapist. Indeed, because of the tenacity of the neurotic's various defense mechanisms, the Primal Therapist must often resort to seemingly crude and ruthless ways to "bust" the patient's defense system, so the pains that have been hidden behind it can be liberated. This is why it is so hard to perform Primal Therapy on oneself: because it is extremely difficult for an individual to go against the "inner emotional grain" to bust his own emotional defense system.

However, in cases of profound personal commitment or severe depression, it is possible for one to get in direct touch with one's repressed feelings without the aid of a Primal Therapist. Although one need not have anyone else present to facilitate the process (the presence of other people can often cause one to become emotionally inhibited), sometimes the quiet presence of a close friend can help to bring out an otherwise elusive repression.

If one is going to attempt to undergo a genuine primal experience on one's own, one must first find a place to go where one can emotionally "let go" without fear of interruption. This is much easier said than done, because people tend to "butt in" whenever they hear someone who is in extreme emotional agony, especially if that person is locked in a darkened room.

Once the proper place has been determined, one simply needs to go there at the peak of one's emotional discomfort, such as during an acute depressive episode. Also, be sure to have a good supply of Kleenex on hand, because it will probably be needed. Once one has been situated in the chosen room, one must then attempt to focus as intensely as possible on the inner *source* of one's pain. Try to zero in on where it is ultimately coming from, no matter how uncomfortable it may happen to be. Although one's inner discomfort will steadily mount as one nears the source of this pain, one can reassure oneself with the knowledge that there will soon come a point where one's discomfort will paradoxically vanish.

This is the point where one suddenly "falls into" the old feeling. Most of one's inner discomfort will cease at this point, because it is the process of defending *against* one's inner pain that causes most of one's painful symptoms. As soon as one ceases resisting the pain and "goes with the flow," one can finally experience the remainder of those feelings that were prematurely terminated long ago.

This is a momentous experience indeed, because it means that one is finally re-connecting with the split-off elements from one's own past. There is an unmistakable sense of ecstasy that is associated with this process, as one joyously becomes reunited with feelings that have been dissociated from consciousness for decades. There is nothing in normal human experience that can quite compare with this extraordinary process of "neurosis in reverse."

Although Janov called his first book *The Primal Scream*, most people only experience prolonged bouts of passionate crying during therapy. The important thing is to simply feel one's old feelings for all they're worth, no matter how agonizing they may happen to be. Again, it always helps to remember that one's subjective level of discomfort will almost certainly go down as soon as one falls into the old feeling.

In order to "catapult" oneself into an old feeling, it sometimes helps to re-create a scene from childhood, or perhaps from a recent dream, in one's mind, so that one can focus on the most emotionally relevant aspects of one's life. For instance, if one has a recurring dream about meeting the father one never had, one can often catapult oneself into the old pain of being fatherless by deliberately focusing on the content of this dream. If there is a friend present during the therapy session, it helps tremendously to describe these emotion-laded scenes to him or her in intimate detail, because the very process of talking about them helps to connect one to the original source of the feeling. There are even times when one has to actually call out to one's parents in agony—even though they're not physically there—in order to enable one to get in touch with one's original feelings.

The most amazing thing about Primal Therapy is that as soon as one relives (i.e., finishes experiencing) an old feeling, the painful effect of it disappears forever. Although the memory of the pain may exist indefinitely, its unpleasant impact on the mind and body is dismantled once and for all when it is fully relived and resolved. This is encouraging news indeed, because it means that we're *not* hopelessly enslaved to those psychological illnesses that we're otherwise powerless to do anything about. It means that we can finally be in control of our own psychological and existential destiny, but *only* if we are committed enough to do what is necessary to become "saved" from ourselves.

# The Existential Lure of the Macho Ideal

THE MACHO IDEAL WOULD NEVER HAVE HAD SUCH A POWERFUL influence over so many men throughout history if it didn't offer a tremendous amount of positive reinforcement to those who espouse it. As we have seen, much of this reinforcement is rooted in the existential fear of mortality that all human beings experience at one time or another. No one wants to be crushed by the many imperfections that are an inherent part of human life. No one wants to see their precious loved ones humiliated by extended suffering and chronic illness. Most importantly, no one wants to see their own miraculous self-consciousness eradicated—seemingly forevermore—by the ever-present scourge of physical death.

When the Macho Ideal is viewed in this light, we see that in many ways it is a direct male reaction to the existential horror that *all* of us tend to experience in the face of our own finitude. This is yet another type of reaction formation, in which our beliefs and attitudes are exactly *opposite* to those that we really and truly possess about life. It's as if the original macho individual were to have said to himself:

> I can't believe that this world is so full of the things that I fear and despise the most. I don't want to deal with all of these miserable imperfections. I don't want to suffer and die. On the contrary, I want to be so strong that I will be totally impervious to all outside threats to my own safety and security. Since I can't actually be this strong immediately, the next best thing I can do is to act in accordance with my existential desire for perfection and immortality whenever I possibly can. Even though I may not yet be this strong, acting *as though* I am will make me feel better overall, since it will help to train me for the eventual attainment of this goal in a million different ways. It will also make me feel better about myself, because it will help me to forget how weak and miserable I really am deep inside.

It is the above attitude that makes it so difficult for many men to give up their belief in the Macho Ideal. For as soon as they recant their belief in its authority over their lives, they suddenly have to face something far more ominous: their twin fears of life and death, which have been suppressed behind their macho defense system from the very beginning. Needless to say, no one wants to stand naked and defenseless in the bitter wind of life's horrendous reality, and this is especially true for Western men, because their very concept of masculinity *requires* them to be strong in the face of all manner of adversity. Since they clearly aren't this strong in and of themselves, they must adopt a false value system (the Macho Ideal) to give them the *illusion* that they are strong enough.

However, regardless of the difficulty of abandoning one's macho defense system, this is nevertheless what must be done if one is to grow beyond the extremely limiting confines of the macho self-image. It would seem that the only way we can do this is by taking Kierkegaard's famous "leap of faith," in which we deliberately allow ourselves to be enriched by our belief in a Higher Power. If we can do this, then it no longer becomes so terrifying to throw away our macho defense system, because we can always fall back on those larger cosmic powers that created us in the first place.

Once this great step in the human developmental process is completed, the way is prepared for a new stage of evolutionary growth as far as the male character structure is concerned. This "man of the 90s" is as different from the old macho man as today's high-tech cars are different from the original Model T. This new type of male is no longer interested in aggression, dominance, and war-related paraphernalia; he is interested, instead, in cleaning up the earth's environment, feeding the world's millions, and helping his own family grow through the many trials and tribulations of modern life.

When we view the meaning of manhood from this novel perspective, we find that the new male transformation we have been discussing is much more than just a simple exercise in psychological and personal development. It is, on the contrary, a transformation that is *absolutely necessary* if our world is to be able to survive into the next century. As you will recall, it is the Macho Ideal that is primarily responsible for generating wars and for mass-producing our modern "genies of death." Thus, if we ever succeed in blowing ourselves up completely, it will be the Macho Ideal that will ultimately be the cause of it (mediated, of course, through human frailty and vulnerability). *This is why the absolute eradication of the Macho Ideal is a goal whose importance is second to none in our world today.*

# The Relative Non-Hostility
# of the French

PARIS HAS LONG BEEN KNOWN AS THE CITY OF ROMANCE. Countless songs and books have been written popularizing the tremendous power of l'amour in this timeless city, and to a large extent this image seems to be correct. Paris is a magical city in many different ways, only one of which is its extreme emphasis on love and romance. One simply has to wander around its many adorable quartiers and broad avenues in order to gain an appreciation for how utterly different Paris is from anything we've ever experienced here in America.

Predictably, this uniqueness even extends to the way in which the French conduct their interpersonal relationships. Not only do they take romance very seriously, they also display attitudes towards the opposite sex that are very different from those typically found in America. This distinction can be seen most notably in the way in which French men tend to regard the female contingent of their society.

In a word, the majority of French men don't seem to experience nearly the amount of hostility toward women that their American counterparts routinely experience. To the contrary, they tend to experience a degree of respect, and even reverence, for femininity that is strangely absent in most American men. This is a peculiar phenomenon indeed, because one might superficially expect "men to be men," no matter where one travels in the world, but such is clearly not the case. This cultural difference in male hostility patterns is consistent with the main thesis of this book, which is that male hostility toward women is largely cultural in origin.

There are several possible explanations for why French men tend to feel comparatively less hostility towards the opposite sex. The chief reason for this difference probably has something to do with the fact that French males are brought up to value femininity and romance from the time they are mere toddlers. American males, on the other hand, are brought up to view women as second-class citizens, whose primary purpose is simply to serve men to the best of their ability.

The French language itself also seems to make a contribution to the relative non-hostility of French males. It is a well-known fact that French is one of the most romantic and "feminine" languages in the entire world. This being the case, one would expect these feminine qualities to naturally have some sort of moderating influence on those who routinely speak French. And so they do. This moderating influence can be witnessed in Parisian parks and neighborhoods, where the "street people" seem more tame and less fearsome than their American counterparts.

This moderating effect is naturally reflected in France's surprisingly low crime rate.[37] Not only are fewer crimes committed per capita in France than in America,[38] the crimes that *are* actually committed are far less vicious and violent on the whole than what we routinely experience here at home. One can actually walk the streets of Paris after midnight without fear of attack, even if one is a woman. Although it is hard to pin down the precise reason for this relatively low crime rate, it undoubtedly has something to do with the vastly different cultural milieu that is found throughout French society.

The French are also much more "artsy" on the whole than we are here in America. French children are taught to appreciate art and literature at a very young age, and this emphasis on creativity is reflected throughout virtually all aspects of French culture. This is immensely important, because the creative arts are rooted primarily in the feminine region of the human psyche, as Swiss psychiatrist C.G. Jung has pointed out. This cultural emphasis on the arts translates into a society that is very receptive towards the feminine aspects of human life, and this in turn helps to keep the problem of male hostility toward women to a minimum.

American culture, on the other hand, is far more masculine in its basic orientation toward life. As a consequence, American males tend to be weaned almost exclusively on a diet of aggressive masculinity from birth, not in conjunction with an appreciation of feminine values, but at the expense of it.

To illustrate, American males are routinely exposed to the aggressive "cowboy" mentality at a very young age. They are given tanks and army men to play with as toddlers; they are shown cartoons on television that are extremely violent; and they are routinely exposed to violent movies, such as *Rambo* and *Robocop*. They are also taught to idolize the game of football, which is one of the most continuously violent sports in existence. When they get a little older, they are further taught to idolize the acquisition of money at all cost, which is a very masculine endeavor by its very nature.

At the same time, though, they are rarely exposed to any of the more feminine aspects of society. In fact, they are verbally *reprimanded* for being interested in anything feminine. A young boy's worst nightmare, for example, is to be called a wimp, sissy, or faggot.

The cumulative effect of these various cultural influences on American males is that they are taught early on to value the ethic of masculinity above all else. Unfortunately, as Jung has pointed out, this undue emphasis on masculinity encourages the development of some of the most destructive personality characteristics in existence, including irrational aggressiveness, stubbornness, combativeness, and the like.

From this point of view, it suddenly becomes easier to understand why American men tend to feel more hostility toward women than their French counterparts: hostility is essentially a masculine type of response; therefore, it is far more likely to occur in a masculine-oriented culture than it is in a feminine-oriented culture.

It would seem to follow, then, that the more masculine one is in one's basic psychological orientation, the more likely one is to become hostile in one's daily life, while the more feminine one is in one's basic orientation, the less likely one is to become hostile. This appears to be a major reason why French men tend to be less hostile overall toward women than their American counterparts: because they have been raised to be far more feminine in their fundamental psychological orientation toward life than American men are.[39]

Being the masculine ethical standard *par excellence*, the Macho Ideal is of course far more compatible with a *masculine* psychological orientation toward life than it is with a feminine orientation. It is for this reason that the Macho Ideal seems to hold so much more power over American men than it does over French men.

However, this isn't to say that French men are not influenced at all by the Macho Ideal. They obviously are, because French society has its own unique set of problems with male chauvinism. Even so, French men don't seem to have nearly as many problems with their machismo as American men do, largely because of the many cultural differences between France and America. These cultural differences tend to generate a preponderance of feminine qualities within the French male psyche, which, as we have seen, tends to moderate any aggressive responses that might be initiated by the Macho Ideal.

Equally important is the apparent fact that French men do not experience nearly the degree of internal or external opposition to the Macho Ideal that American men tend to experience. This is significant, because it means that the macho inclinations that *are* experienced by French men do not tend to be opposed as strongly by French women or by French society in general. This produces less hostility overall, because as we have seen, hostility reactions in men are directly related to two distinct factors: 1) the degree to which a given individual is influenced by the Macho Ideal, and 2) the amount of anti-macho counterattack a macho individual experiences in his daily life.

All things being equal, then, we would expect more hostility out of a macho-oriented man whose macho beliefs are aggressively challenged than out of the same type of individual whose macho beliefs are *not* challenged. This would explain much of the reason for the relative non-hostility of the French, since certain aspects of the Macho Ideal are not as vigorously opposed in French society as they are in American society.

To illustrate, the French don't find marital infidelity to be nearly as distasteful as Americans tend to find it. It is not uncommon, for instance, for a French man to have a wife *and* at least one mistress. Although such situations may not be totally without adverse effect, they are nevertheless much better tolerated by the French than by Americans. In America, adulterous acts often lead to outright divorce, and even when they don't, the quality of the marital relationship tends to deteriorate once the adultery is discovered, even if no more philandering ever takes place. In France, on the other hand, adulterous acts in and of themselves *rarely* lead to divorce. They also don't tend to harm French marriages to the same extent as they do American marriages.

Part of the reason for this curious phenomenon may be that the French simply idolize romance to such a degree that they can't help but maximize their romantic experiences whenever they possibly can, even if it means routinely pursuing extramarital affairs. And since both the man *and* the woman often tend to crave extramarital affairs equally, both are more likely than their American counterparts to forgive each other whenever adultery is engaged in. In America, on the other hand, it is usually the man who wants to have an extramarital affair, and it is usually the woman who opposes it (though this is certainly less true today than it was in the past).

Moreover, the physical act of adultery is considered much more heinous here in America than it is in France. As a consequence, whenever an American man commits an adulterous act, his wife is typically *not* as forgiving of him as a French woman would be in the same circumstance. This means that the would-be American philanderer faces a tremendous amount of potential opposition to his macho inclinations if he chooses to give in to them. Indeed, this opposition may explain much of the reason why American males tend to react with such hostility whenever they are caught engaging in adulterous behavior.

French society as a whole also tends to be much more tolerant of adulterous behavior than American society. This relaxing of societal standards as far as adultery is concerned means that French men can give in to their philanderous urgings without facing an extreme amount of societal opposition. This in turn translates into less of a potential for overt hostility reactions in French men, because it means that their macho inclinations aren't being opposed intensely enough in this one area to warrant a significant hostility response.

Another area where the Macho Ideal in France is not opposed as vigorously as it is here in the United States is in the area of interpersonal aggression between husband and wife (or equally, between lovers). While there may be less interpersonal aggression overall in France than in America, it still occurs, and to the extent that it does occur, it is generally allowed to proceed uninterrupted by the police (unless serious harm seems to be in the immediate offing), unlike it is in America. This socially-sanctioned ability for a man to "be a man" is in direct accordance with the dictates of the Macho Ideal, which state that a man should have the power to conduct his romantic affairs in any way he sees fit. This being the case, French men tend to experience less societal opposition to this particular aspect of the Macho Ideal, which in turn means that they tend to experience less hostility overall towards women.

American men (and women), on the other hand, often perceive that their romantic affairs are being monitored by the Establishment so closely that they don't feel completely free to do as they please. For men, this externally-derived opposition to the Macho Ideal constitutes yet another reason for a substantial hostility reaction toward women, since macho men who are not allowed to act out their machismo typically become aggressive and sometimes even violent as a response.

Of course, this isn't to say that men should be allowed to act in unrestricted accordance with the dictates of the Macho Ideal. It is simply to say that as long as men possess a macho ethical standard deep inside, they will be less prone to developing hostility reactions if external opposition to their macho standards is held to a minimum. Ideally, though, men should abandon the Macho Ideal *altogether*, so that they will no longer be in possession of a macho standard that can be opposed. This is the only sure-fire way to overcome the hostility trap in macho men once and for all.

### French Sexism vs. American Sexism

In many ways France is still a very sexist country, as are most European countries of Latin descent. French men and women tend to interact with one another as *men* and *women*, and not simply as people.

That is to say, there is still a strong sexual component at work in French male-female relations, even if it isn't always directly acted upon. French women on the whole *want* to be desired as women, and they aren't afraid to dress and act in such a way as to let that fact be publicly known. French men, of course, are only too happy to accommodate them in this capacity, so both sexes tend to act in a mutually satisfying way towards one another. The result of this overtly sexist means of interpersonal behavior is an exciting social ambience where passion and romance are typically the "rule the day."

The big difference, however, between the type of sexism practiced in France and that practiced in the United States is that in France, a woman's career does *not* have to suffer because of her open delight in being a woman. French women have access to most of the same careers and social opportunities that their American counterparts have, yet they don't feel compelled to sacrifice any aspect of their womanhood in order to obtain it. They can dress and act as sexy and as flashy as they want, *and they don't have to pay an inordinate professional price for it.* In other words, the possibility of career advancement for a French woman isn't typically seen as being mutually exclusive with her being a "real" woman, who can play directly into traditional sexist roles.

In America, on the other hand, many women feel compelled to give up a certain amount of their native "womanhood" in order to be able to climb up the corporate ladder. Part of the reason for this seems to be the inconsiderateness and outright vulgarity that is often displayed by American males. Since these abusive men don't usually know how to deal with professional women who simultaneously take pride in their own sexuality, American women tend to react by being more conservative in the degree of sexuality that they reflect to the outside world, especially if they are trying to work their way up the corporate ladder.

In many ways Americans have perverted much of the old world charm that still exists between men and women in other countries. Since a sizable proportion of American men don't know how to treat women with the care and respect they deserve in life, American women tend to feel compelled to take appropriate countermeasures in order to protect themselves. The end result of this mutual alteration of the traditional male-female relationship is a good deal of hostility and resentment on the part of both sexes. American women resent the almost constant mistreatment that they tend to receive from men; they also resent being forced to retract so much of their womanhood in order to be able to get ahead in the business world.

American men, on the other hand, resent the many changes that they've had to accept over the years on the part of these newly "liberated" women, even though it was originally the male segment of society who made most of these changes necessary in the first place. They resent having to deal with women who have largely removed themselves from the "circle of influence" of the Macho Ideal. This in turn tends to lead straight to an outright hostility response on the part of these macho individuals, for as we have seen, overly macho men tend to react with hostility whenever their underlying masculine standard is confronted or contradicted by others.

In the end, there really isn't any such thing as "sexism" or "sexual liberation" *per se*. There is only a respectful or disrespectful way of dealing with the opposite sex. If American men could only behave in a respectful and honorable way towards women, they wouldn't have to compel so many women to "liberate" themselves in order to get ahead, because the women themselves would *already* be liberated by such a radical change in male behavior.

### Other Forms of the Macho Ideal

To participate in some form of the Macho Ideal isn't *necessarily* to think or behave in a derogatory fashion toward women. Although in this book we have concentrated on a *single* Macho Ideal (because it is the prevalent one in the United States), the fact is that there are *other* types of Macho Ideals to be found throughout the world. And while they may share some characteristics with the American version, in some instances they can be radically different.

The French Macho Ideal, for example, is much less concerned with power and superiority over women than it is here in America. To the contrary, it concerned primarily with the ability to pursue love and romance to the greatest possible extent in society. But French women *also* share this concern for romance to a similar degree. Thus, this romantic behavioral ethic in and of itself barely qualifies as being "macho" at all. It only becomes macho when men want to exert *undue force* in having their own way in life.

### Middle Eastern Chauvinism vs. American Chauvinism

During the Gulf War in Iraq, millions of Americans learned about the severe male chauvinism that exists throughout the Middle East. In comparison with these male-dominated countries, the United States superficially seems like an enlightened, progressive place. And in many ways it is. Women here don't have to wear shawls over their faces, they can drive, and they can have bank accounts. They can even go to the very top of the professional or business world.

However, it would be a mistake to conclude that the chauvinism of the Middle East is *that* much worse than it is here. It isn't. It just *seems* to be that way because it is much more up front. In many ways, the chauvinism we have here in America is just as bad as it is in the Middle East, and in some ways it's actually worse. It's just not as visible because it's conducted "under the table," so to speak, in a very hidden and subtle fashion.

On the surface, it seems as though American males have been liberated from the oppressive restraints imposed by the Macho Ideal, since women *seem* to have so much freedom and equality in this country. The fact is, however, that the majority of American men still pledge allegiance to the Macho Ideal just as strongly as their Middle Eastern counterparts do; they just choose to deal with it in different ways.

Middle Eastern men tend to openly act in accordance with their version of the Macho Ideal, and the majority of Middle Eastern women tend accept this inferior social and personal status without significant opposition. By doing it openly, though, Middle Eastern men don't put excessive psychological strain on themselves, since they are directly acting in response to the macho code of ethics that they are holding deep inside.

American men, on the other hand, believe in more or less the *same* Macho Ideal, but they are prevented from openly acting upon it (at least in a completely unopposed fashion) by the "liberated" social structure that exists in this country. However, since they still believe in this macho standard every bit as strongly as Middle Eastern men do, they are forced to go "underground," so to speak, with their chauvinist feelings and attitudes by expressing them through more covert channels. This suppression of the macho response in turn generates a *tremendous* amount of psychopathology in American men, the majority of which is directed towards the opposite sex.

The eminent psychologist Carl Rogers has noted that any incongruence between a person's inner feelings and outer behavior is pathological by definition. It is pathological because it puts excessive strain on a person's overall psychological status, which in turn forces the mind to become distended at its weakest point.

Macho-oriented American men tend to suffer from precisely this type of incongruence as far as the opposite sex is concerned. Though they inwardly believe that men are superior to women, they try to outwardly act as if women are equally important citizens of society. This incongruence produces varying degrees of psychopathology in susceptible males, which in extreme cases can manifest itself in wife beating, rape, or even outright murder.

These violent crimes against women are far less common in the Middle East, probably because the men there are not forcing themselves to act in a way that contradicts their inner set of beliefs. The solution, of course, is not for American society to become as openly chauvinistic as Middle Easterner society is, but for American men to do away with the Macho Ideal altogether, so that their inner thoughts and feelings will no longer contradict their expected outer behavior.

### Male Hostility and the Struggle to Perform

As Warren Farrell has pointed out in his best-selling book *Why Men Are The Way They Are*, American men tend to experience a phenomenal amount of culturally-induced pressure to perform well on the job. Although the feminist movement has served to remove some of this enormous pressure, men are *still* expected to do well in the financial sphere, even if it means sacrificing a large part of their health and well-being in order to do so. Indeed, this situation has gotten so out of hand in America that the perceived attractiveness of any given male, especially in terms of marriage, is often directly related to his degree of financial success on the job. The more financially successful he is, the more attractive he tends to be perceived, not only by others, but also by himself as well.

One need only travel overseas to see how desperate this situation has become in America. In France, for example, a man's perceived degree of attractiveness and desirability has relatively little to do with how much money he makes or with what type of job he has (to a point, of course). Instead, he tends to be evaluated, both by himself and by others, in terms of *who he is in and of himself*. This is an incredibly important distinction, because the degree of hostility that is experienced by both men and women in a society seems to be directly related to the process by which an individual's self-worth is evaluated in that society.

In the United States, for instance, most men tend to take it for granted that their self-worth is largely defined by what kind of job they have and by how much money they make.[40] In France, on the other hand, it is actually considered to be *poor taste* for a man to tell a new acquaintance what he does for a living (unless, of course, he is directly asked). Instead, the emphasis is on who a man *is*, on what kind of personality he has, and on what kind of conversation he can maintain.

The type of job one has or the amount of money one makes obviously has very little, if anything, to do with these personal qualities in and of themselves. This is why American men often seem so shallow to foreigners: because they have emphasized their careers over virtually everything else in their lives, and their personalities have correspondingly suffered as a result.

Needless to say, it doesn't feel very good to constantly neglect one's true inner self in favor of one's career. In fact, this kind of experience can be downright degrading and even humiliating because in the end, all we ever really have is our own selves, not our jobs or our money. This is another major reason why American men are so susceptible to feelings of hostility, and even rage: because it is only natural for their innermost selves to fight back when they find that they are being suffocated day by day in the constant pursuit of money and prestige.

As Carl Jung has so eloquently pointed out, the deepest goal of human life is for *individuation*; that is, for the personality to grow into a mature, self-actualized form. This goal is so important that Jung even postulated the existence of a built-in "individuation drive" in humans to help bring it about. However, as long as our innermost self is repeatedly being stifled by our complete commitment to being "successful" at all cost, we can't hope to make much progress towards our species-based goal of self-actualization.

It is a well-known fact, however, that when *any* built-in drive is suffocated in a person's life, that drive automatically tends to fight back in order to reassert itself. If, for instance, we attempt to stifle our physical drive to breathe, we will start gasping for air in just a few seconds. Similarly, if we attempt to stifle our built-in psychological drive for self-actualization, we will inevitably become hostile and aggressive as a result.

This seems to be yet another reason why French men tend to experience so much less hostility overall than their American counterparts: because their real selves aren't getting choked as severely by an unrealistic devotion to money and "success."

### Hostility and the Arts

As we have seen throughout this chapter, it would be a mistake to underestimate the profound influence a society can have on the amount of hostility its citizens tend to feel in life. The way a society is set up can almost single-handedly determine how its citizens will feel in their day-to-day lives. This is particularly true of the *value system* that a society perpetrates upon its people.

**104**

In America, for instance, money is much more important from a societal point of view than the arts. Artists of all kinds tend to be looked upon with relative derision when compared to doctors, lawyers, and business executives; that is, unless they happen to become "successful" at their work and make a lot of money. This emphasis on financial success even finds its way into the streets and thoroughfares of modern-day America, as people with money tend to openly flaunt it, because it tends to bring them greater respect and admiration.

In France, on the other hand, things are quite different. Not only are the arts held in much higher esteem than they are here in America, when people *do* have a lot of money, they tend to *not* show it off, so as to not appear to be distasteful, or even downright vulgar. This relative emphasis on the arts has the curious effect of giving the French an added dimension in the perpetual human quest for being happy and fulfilled in life. No matter how poor and miserable a French person may be (short of actually starving to death, of course), he or she still can still resort to the arts in order to obtain a significant amount of culturally-sanctioned pleasure.

In Paris, for example, it isn't uncommon to find dirt-poor individuals spontaneously breaking out into song in the street, and this is largely an accepted means of personal expression in public. In America, such an act would be looked upon as contemptible evidence of mental instability.

It is a well-known fact that artistic expression provides a great release for pent-up nervous tension and other forms of psychological stress. A tremendous amount of "steam" can be released simply by engaging in some form of creative endeavor, or by reflecting on someone else's creative act. It follows from this relation that the arts can provide an important "safety valve" for the venting of an entire population's feelings of anger and hostility, but only if the arts are made freely available to everyone.

All in all, the cumulative effect of France's societal emphasis on the arts is that its citizens seem to have an extra buffer zone separating them from absolute despair. As a consequence of this added dimension, they tend to feel less hostile and violent overall than their American counterparts, and this in spite of the fact that it is extremely difficult to make an adequate living in Paris these days. This decreased propensity for aggression is reflected in France's comparatively low violent crime rate.

# Conclusion

THROUGHOUT THIS BOOK, WE HAVE SPOKEN OF THE MACHO IDEAL as being an integral part of all patriarchal societies. To some people, this may seem to connote a certain degree of hopelessness and helplessness regarding the ability of macho males to escape the influence of this value standard.

Fortunately, although the effects of the Macho Ideal are *extremely* pervasive and affect both males and females alike in countless ways, being raised in a patriarchal society does *not* necessarily condemn a man to a mindless belief in this macho-oriented system of ethics. With sufficient "consciousness-raising," it is possible for macho males to overcome their slavish devotion to the "cause of masculinity" that they were raised to believe in.

This kind of self-transformation, however, doesn't come easy. It takes a lot of pain and hard work to overcome the years of macho indoctrination that men in our society have been faced with since they were infants. It also takes a good deal of courage, because it is a fearful thing indeed for a person to deliberately leave the precious comfort of the "herd" for a new type of value system.

This difficulty is compounded by the fact that we aren't talking about merely changing political parties or about converting to a new religion. *We're talking about changing the most deeply influential thing in a man's life: his underlying value system, through which he derives his very identity as a man.*

It isn't easy to change the underlying content of this system, because in order to do so, one must temporarily *give up* the contents of one's previous value system. This means—or at least seems to mean—temporarily giving up all of the most important things in a man's life, and most men are understandably loathe to do that. This is especially true as far as far as a man's innermost identity as a man is concerned. Since the macho male derives most of his identity as a man from his psychological identification with the Macho Ideal, he feels like he will be risking his very identity as a human being if he gives up these precious value standards. Yet, give them up he must if he is to completely change his psychological orientation, because his old value system clearly must die before a new one can take its place.

It helps tremendously if the macho male can be brought to understand that he won't be losing his ultimate identity as a human being if he chooses to eliminate the Macho Ideal from his life. He is simply shedding his pathological macho identity in favor of a *new* identity that is much healthier and more consistent with what true masculinity is all about.

In other words, since the Macho Ideal is a false description of human masculinity, the man who believes in it isn't a "real man" after all. In order to become a "real man," then, the macho individual must first shed this false ethical standard in favor of a more realistic description of human masculinity. If the macho individual can be brought to realize this, the process of personal transformation will be made *much* easier, because he will then understand that he is about to embark on the most important and masculine journey of all: the journey of becoming a *real* man.

What is most needed to help bring about this personal transformation is hope and encouragement: hope that there is indeed light at the end of the tunnel, and encouragement that one can truly succeed at this venture if one simply tries hard enough to do so. As always, the more personal education that one can receive in this area the better, because education means awareness, and awareness is what any kind of self-transformation is all about.

### The Intrinsic Evil of the Macho Ideal

As we have seen throughout this book, the Macho Ideal is, in one way or another, responsible for causing the vast majority of pain and suffering on this planet. It has incited men to go to war with each other and to brutally kill millions, perhaps even billions, of innocent people. It has caused untold numbers of men to beat their wives, to rape innocent women, and to tragically abuse their own children and other people's children. In recent years, it has even gone so far as to cause the progressive destruction of our own precious environment, just as it has also brought the entire world to the brink of total annihilation.

Without a doubt, then, the Macho Ideal must constitute one of the greatest evils that has ever been seen on this planet. Unfortunately, though, because it cannot be directly seen, smelled, touched, or heard (i.e., because it is not a material object), it is a very hard thing for most people to become aware of. This awareness is crucial, however, if the evil of the Macho Ideal is to ever be done away with in our society.

Given the profound destructiveness of the Macho Ideal throughout human history, along with the ridiculous, prehistoric nature of its basic suppositions, there is no question that it is completely and utterly mistaken. The fact that it was originally based on a few incidental aspects of our anatomy and physiology should not deter us from reaching this conclusion, because the phenomenon of male superiority is most definitely *not* an inevitable part of the natural order. For as we have seen, the Macho Ideal is *not* the direct (and, therefore, inevitable) consequence of how we are physically constructed. It is, rather, the *indirect* result of how our prehistoric ancestors originally chose to *interpret* the facts of their own anatomy.

Thus, the question we now need to ask ourselves is this: Do we want to continue living our lives according to a badly outmoded value system that was established in prehistoric times by people who were almost completely ignorant of the implications of their own behavior? Or, do we want to extricate ourselves from this poisonous pedagogy once and for all, so that we can move on to a more sophisticated and appropriate value system that is more productive for the entire planet? *Due to the timeless relationship between war and male hostility, the future of our entire planet clearly rests on how we as a species will choose to answer this all-important question.*

# Notes

1. Statistics provided by Sue Julian and Paula Bickman of the West Virginia Coalition Against Domestic Violence.

2. The present discussion is not meant to cover the development of all societies, because not all societies have been centered around men. A good many matriarchal societies have existed as well. Hence, the present discussion can only be properly applied to those ancient societies that developed in a patriarchal fashion, not to all ancient societies in general.

3. Cambridge University physicist Stephen Hawking provides a good example of the non-correlation between personal competence and physical strength. Hawking is said to be the world's greatest living scientific genius, yet he is confined to a wheelchair because he is completely paralyzed by Lou Gherig's Disease.

4. Sanford, *The Kingdom Within*, 21.

5. This would explain a possible reason for the existence of two separate genders in the first place: insofar as the physical differences between the sexes actually facilitates the existence of a corresponding set of psychological differences between them, a multifaceted human psyche containing both masculine and feminine qualities would seem to exclusively require the existence of a two-gendered world, as opposed to a single-gendered one.

6. The first way in which macho men are fraudulent, you may recall, is that they outwardly pretend to love women, when in fact they hate them with a passion.

7. Males who have been castrated experience little or no sexual desire, because they no longer have sufficient blood levels of testosterone to get them sexually excited. However, once they receive an injection of testosterone, they are able to experience sexual desire almost immediately.

8. In the case of rape, and other forms of male sexual violence against women, males use their physical power to overwhelm the female's intrinsic prerogative to choose that normally applies during peacetime.

9. Once excited, however, women tend to be far more competent and longer-lasting in bed than men are. In the popular vernacular, it is the "quick-shooter" who tends to quickly poop himself out, while it is the slow and steady builder who can last all night.

10. There may be a teleological (i.e. goal-oriented) reason for this relatively late peaking of the female sex drive. Since a woman's biological "window" for conception begins to close around the age of forty, there are definite time constraints for determining when she can and cannot get pregnant. Thus if it is one of the goals of life that females should bear as many children as they can, then a mechanism must be found for increasing the likelihood of pregnancy before the biological window of conception snaps completely shut. A greatly increased sex drive during the third decade of life is the perfect mechanism for allowing this to occur.

11. Masters and Johnson, *Human Sexual Response*.

12. It would seem, then, that the archetype of the whore or slut is a direct response to the sexual dictates of the Macho Ideal, which work together to determine what type of woman the macho individual finds sexually attractive. Of course, this is just another way of saying that the macho desire for sluttiness is largely a culturally learned trait, and not necessarily an inborn trait that all "real" men share.

13. Dahlberg, "On Lust," *Reasons of the Heart*.

14. In cases of equal opportunity, however, men still seem to be more philanderous overall than women. One reason for this apparent fact (which appears to be becoming less and less true with the passage of time) would seem to be that women appear to be more emotionally committed to the idea of monogamy than men.

15. Nimkoff, *Comparative Family Systems*, 17.

16. Of course, not all men who subscribe to the dictates of the Macho Ideal believe that men have the God-given right to be polygamous. They just have a greater overall tendency to do so, given their unmitigated belief in male superiority.

17. Goldberg, *The Hazards of Being Male*, 13.

18. Ibid., 13.

19. Ibid., 12.

20. Forward and Torres, *Men Who Hate Women & the Women Who Love Them*.

21. Ibid., 99-100.

22. Layden, *Escaping The Hostility Trap*.

23. Starke, "Wife Abuse in the Medical Setting: An Introduction to Health Personnel."

24. Browne and Williams, "Resource Availability for Women at Risk: Its Relationship to Rates of Female-Perpetrated Partner Homicide."

25. Forward and Torres, *Men Who Hate Women & The Women Who Love Them*, 121-122.

26. Sanford, *The Invisible Partners*, 3.

27. Berdyaev, *The Destiny of Man*, 61-62.

28. Beebe, *Aspects of the Masculine R.F.C.*, xiii.

29. Jung, *Aspects of the Masculine*, xi.

30. It is not too much to claim that emotional stress can simultaneously cause physical problems in the young child. It is now a well-known fact that there is a direct link between the mind's emotional center and the physical status of the body. Indeed, an exciting new medical discipline, known as psychoneuroimmunology, has sprung up in recent years to study this very phenomenon.

31. Roger Waters, originally of the rock group Pink Floyd, has symbolically referred to this type of psychological barrier as "the wall." He even wrote an entire rock opera (also called "The Wall") around this important psychological device.

32. Of course, not all people fall in love in this manner, because it is neurotic by definition, and not all people are susceptible to neurotic entanglements. It is possible to love people for who they really are, instead of who they unconsciously remind us of, and indeed, there are many people who would argue that this type of non-neurotic love is the only genuine kind of love there really is.

33. The same general principles can be applied to *all* monogamous relationships, regardless of whether a formal marriage has taken place or not.

34. Levine, *Antioxidant Adaptation: Its Role in Free Radical Pathology*.

35. Layden, *Escaping the Hostility Trap*, 28-41.

36. Indeed, the belief that one is intrinsically inferior as a human being is, in a very real way, the greatest possible insult that one can deliver to the Cosmic Power that created us.

37. Whitcomb, "Safe Streets: What Other Nations Do: Paris," *The Christian Science Monitor*.

38. "Trends in Crime Rates," *A National Strategy To Reduce Crime*, 12-20.

39. It should be noted that a man with a feminine psychological orientation is not necessarily the same thing as an effeminate man. An effeminate man is a woman-like individual who is very likely to be gay. A man with a strong feminine orientation, on the other hand, is simply more likely to value such desirable qualities as creativeness, harmony, love, and the like; it doesn't necessarily mean that he is woman-like, or any less desirable as a "man."

40. This is one reason why so many foreigners tend to perceive Americans as being too tough, too superficial, and too hung up on money.

# References

Becker, Ernest. *The Denial of Death*. New York: The Free Press, 1973.

Berdyaev, Nicholas. *The Destiny of Man*. New York: Harper Torchbooks, 1960.

Browne, A. and K. R. Williams. "Resource Availability for Women at Risk: Its Relationship to Rates of Female-Perpetrated Partner Homicide." Paper presented at the American Society of Criminology Annual Meeting, Montreal, Canada. November 11-14, 1987.

Corey, Michael A. *Why Men Cheat: Psychological Profiles of the Adulterous Male*. Springfield, IL: Charles C. Thomas, Publisher, 1989.

Farrell, Warren. *Why Men Are the Way They Are*. New York: McGraw-Hill, 1986.

Forward, Susan, and Joan Torres. *Men Who Hate Women & the Women Who Love Them*. New York: Bantam Books, 1987.

Goldberg, Herb. *The Hazards of Being Male*. New York: New American Library, 1976.

Hall, Calvin S., and Gardner Lindzey. *Theories of Personality*. New York: John Wiley & Sons, 1978.

Hite, Shere. *The Hite Report on Male Sexuality*. New York: Ballantine Books, 1981.

Janov, Arthur. *The Primal Revolution*. New York: Simon & Schuster, 1972.

————. *The Primal Scream*. New York: The Putnam Publishing Group, 1981.

Johnson, Robert A. *We: Understanding Masculine Psychology* (San Francisco: Harper & Row, 1974).

————. *We: Understanding the Psychology of Romantic Love*. San Francisco: Harper & Row, 1983.

Jung, C. G. *Aspects of the Masculine*. Translated by R.F.C. Hull. Princeton: Princeton University Press, 1989.

Layden, Milton. *Escaping the Hostility Trap*. Englewood Cliffs: Prentice-Hall, 1977.

Levine, Stephen A., with Parris M. Kidd. *Antioxidant Adaptation: Its Role in Free Radical Pathology*. San Leandro, CA: Biocurrents, 1985.

Masters, William H., and Virginia E. Johnson. *Human Sexual Inadequacy*. Boston: Little, Brown, and Co., 1970.

———— *Human Sexual Response*. Boston: Little, Brown, and Co., 1966.

————. *The Pleasure Bond*.Boston: Little, Brown, and Co., 1974.

Nimkoff, M. F., ed. *Comparative Family Systems*. Boston: Houghton Mifflin, 1965.

Phares, E. Jerry. *Clinical Psychology*. Homewood, IL: The Dorsey Press, 1979.

Sanford, John A. *The Invisible Partners*. New York: Paulist Press, 1980.

————. *The Kingdom Within*. San Francisco: Harper & Row, 1987.

Starke, E. "Wife Abuse in the Medical Setting: An Introduction to Health Personnel," Monograph Series No. 7, National Clearinghouse on Domestic Violence, Washington, D.C.: U.S. Government Printing Office, April, 1981.

# Index